McGraw-Hill's

CAREERS FOR

NATURE LOVERS

& Other Outdoor Types

Careers for You Series

McGraw-Hill's

CAREERS FOR

NATURE LOVERS

& Other Outdoor Types

LOUISE MILLER

THIRD EDITION

New York   Chicago   San Francisco   Lisbon   London   Madrid   Mexico City
Milan   New Delhi   San Juan   Seoul   Singapore   Sydney   Toronto

The *McGraw·Hill* Companies

Library of Congress Cataloging-in-Publication Data

Miller, Louise.
    Careers for nature lovers & other outdoor types / by Louise Miller — 3rd ed.
        p.   cm. — (McGraw-Hill careers for you series)
        ISBN 0-07-148218-0 (alk. paper)
        1. Conservation of natural resources—Vocational guidance.
        2. Environmental protection—Vocational guidance.   3. Biology—Vocational
        guidance   I. Title.

        S945.M55 2008
        333.72023—dc22   2007010790

1 2 3 4 5 6 7 8 9 10 11 12 13 14 15   DOC/DOC   0 9 8 7

ISBN 978-0-07-148218-9
MHID   0-07-148218-0

McGraw-Hill books are available at special quantity discounts to use as premiums and
sales promotions, or for use in corporate training programs. For more information,
please write to the Director of Special Sales, Professional Publishing, McGraw-Hill,
Two Penn Plaza, New York, NY 10121-2298. Or contact your local bookstore.

This book is printed on acid-free paper.

Contents

Preface

They say the first step in choosing the right career is to focus on what you really want. If you're set on a life of working outdoors, you're already on the right track with this guide. You can use it to explore several options and further focus your efforts with job descriptions, curriculum recommendations, pros and cons of the work, career outlooks, salary estimates, and resources for additional information. Before you're finished, you should have a good sense of whether these types of jobs are for you.

Each chapter addresses a different field; some are interrelated, and some have a charm all their own. Bioscientists (Chapter 2) study and manage plants, animals, or ecosystems. Conservationists (Chapter 3) such as foresters and range managers monitor a specific resource and reconcile human needs with natural ones. Agricultural specialists (Chapter 4) work in many areas, from soil management to food safety, and might also be bioscientists and conservationists at the same time. Their responsibilities include delivering safe foods to market, maximizing yield and efficiency, and protecting the land and water that make it possible.

Land planners and landscape architects (Chapter 5) approach things from a different perspective. Both literally shape the land, seeking its best use in people-oriented environments. Planners, whether addressing an entire cityscape or an isolated tract, analyze usage patterns and navigate zoning, building codes, assorted regulations, and environmental impacts to shepherd projects to completion. Landscape architects incorporate aspects of landscaping, architecture, and planning in their work. Geoscientists (Chapter 6) study the nonliving elements of the earth, from the material (rock, water, oil) to the intangible (climate, magnetic fields). Some, such as certain types of oceanographers, are considered bioscientists *and* geoscientists. Finally, pollution control specialists (Chapter 7) reduce people's impact on the environment by testing and processing the waste from our industrialized society, from wastewater to heavy toxins. More so than the others, this field presents opportunities for people of all educational levels.

For many of the other jobs covered here, especially among the scientific positions, education is paramount. Master's degrees and doctorates are standard, and the enhanced pay generally reflects that additional schooling. Even so, perhaps the best benefit of all is the substantive relationships that outdoor professionals have with the natural world, which keeps them intimately familiar with its pace, character, and purpose. That interplay can take you back to the human race's deepest roots, even as you wield high-tech equipment in the field.

None of the jobs really calls for a specific brand of politics, but many of them will be most attractive to the environmentalist, the thinker who recognizes that our quality of life depends on the health of everything around us and desires to improve both. Other jobs simply call for someone with a robust understanding of a portion of the earth or the life it supports. Either type of person will benefit from a life lived out-of-doors, something that's far too novel these days, as they make discoveries both personal and professional in their daily work. And if, in reading through this guide, you find these paths are not for you, you'll still have made an important discovery.

Acknowledgments

The author would like to thank Brad Crawford for his assistance in preparing this edition.

CHAPTER ONE

The World Is Your Office

Too many people have a workday routine that borders on desperate. They commute to work on traffic-clogged interstates five days a week, or more, and spend most of their eight- to ten-hour days at a computer, bathed in fluorescent light and adrift in a sea of cubicles. Maybe they steal away for an hour at lunch or for a quick chat around the watercooler, and maybe ten years down the line they'll get promoted to an office with a door.

Either way, too rarely will they breathe fresh air, know the simple joy of physical exertion, and come to understand the natural world on its terms. We are not so removed from our heritage of agriculture and exploration that we can be entirely content with sedentary, virtual lives. There is another way.

So many of us have become estranged from the realities of life on Earth that we require ambassadors—scientists, guardians, planners, pollution specialists, and others—to venture out into the real world and tell us what's actually going on. They are the ones with their fingers on the pulse, the ones who know the meaning behind the numbers and the true impact of our actions on the environment. We rely on their know-how much more than we realize: in preserving soils for farming, bringing healthy crops and farm animals to market, purifying and treating our water, charting long-term climate trends, monitoring potential natural disasters, and much else. For that elite corps of outdoor ambassadors, the world is their office, and, refreshingly, their schedule depends more on the nature of the job than on time clocks.

A New Sense of Urgency

For decades, we heard proclamations of impending doom for the environment. Whales, dolphins, spotted owls, chestnuts, wolves, rain forests, rhinos. Love Canal, Chernobyl, Three Mile Island, the Exxon *Valdez*. Each battle or catastrophe got framed as an apocalyptic confrontation of good versus evil, with both sides wearying of the continual name calling and stakes raising. For the most part, environmental groups have since recognized that fear is not an effective long-term tool of persuasion and that not every political loss will bring about our demise. Our fate, positive or negative, will be the result of collective action applied one person at a time over years, decades, and centuries, driven by a commitment to the common good and often at the expense of short-term, personal gains.

Such a prudent approach is not nearly as catchy, however, and people are reluctant to make sweeping life changes based on abstract concepts. The key to motivating change is information—hard, objective data from experts who can make the situation concrete and convey with a sense of optimism what people can do to make it better. Environmental, political, and economic circumstances have already combined to remind us all that the status quo isn't working. Global warming is probably the most daunting ecological challenge we've ever faced as people, and many, particularly those with commercial interests to protect, refuse even to acknowledge it as a product of human creation. Racing population growth has punctuated our extremely limited freshwater supplies (which are often contaminated), while new affluence and industrialization in developing countries foreshadows a looming energy crisis. Coral reefs are dying, and species worldwide continue to disappear at an astonishing rate. We have much to overcome, and through observation, analysis, and public education, outdoors professionals will be a first line of defense in counteracting the stresses we place on the world. If the world is the office of outdoor professionals, then their jobs must be to keep the office running smoothly.

Where You Fit In

Your professional life and career goals *can* be compatible with the best interests of the larger world. If you are in school now, start thinking seriously about courses you should take and adjust your curriculum accordingly. Talk to career counselors, look at the websites of relevant professional organizations and government departments (we include a healthy list in the Appendix), and talk to professionals in the fields you're interested in whenever you have a chance, even if you don't plan on starting a career for several years. Most people are enthusiastic about discussing their jobs and will be flattered that you've taken an interest, so don't be afraid to make a few calls and request informational interviews or a career-shadowing visit. You might just gain a future reference or valuable sounding board.

Most important, search yourself. Think about what the types of activities you most enjoy doing, what you're best at, and the lifestyle you'd like to have. Some basic questions will help determine the environmental career that's right for you:

1. Do you enjoy being outdoors, even in less than perfect weather?
2. If so, what is it about the outdoors that attracts you?
3. Do you gravitate toward plants, animals, or the landscape itself?
4. How much time, money, and effort are you willing to dedicate to your education?
5. Are you an observer or an analyzer? Are you an introvert or an extrovert? Are you a big-picture thinker or more detail oriented?
6. Do you prefer to work independently or as part of a team?

Since the outdoor world provides you with a variety of career opportunities, you will have to make decisions based on your answers to these questions. Take a minute now to jot down your thoughts, and keep your responses handy as you look through the subsequent chapters to see how they fit with the career descriptions. Many jobs are performed outdoors, sometimes in the worst kind of weather. Some jobs require physical strength and fitness. Others require a great deal of education and training. All those factors and many others may determine which career you will choose.

Career assessment tests, such as the Myers-Briggs Type Indicator (www.myersbriggs.org) or Focus (www.focuscareer.com), an inventory of interests and values, can help reinforce hunches or present career paths you wouldn't otherwise have considered. They are by no means the final authority on what kind of job is right for you, but they can be useful tools. Often these tests are available online with professional consultation for a fee.

If you are changing careers, you will also have to assess your strengths and interests. You will have to determine the specific field you want to be in and the extent of education and training you will need. It may take a few years of night school to acquire the certificate, license, or degree that you need, but the time and effort will be well worth it when you're finally doing work you love.

So what are these career options we're talking about? Of course all manner of jobs could call for work in the out-of-doors: tour group leaders, theme park staff, and lifeguards, just to name a few. What we've focused on here are jobs that foster a connection to the land or natural world or that require our interaction with it on a fundamental level.

The Biosciences

If we define biology as the study of living things, we can see how all-encompassing careers in the biological sciences can be. They include everything from aquatic biologists to soil scientists, from botanists to toxicologists, from game managers to horticulturists. Biologists are employed in forests and agricultural research stations and on ocean ships and farms. If you choose biology for a career, you will need at least a bachelor's degree. A master's or doctoral degree can ensure more opportunities and is the ticket to a durable career. So start studying now to be a botanist, physiologist, biochemist, zoologist, ecologist, or horticulturist, and you will enter the wonderful world of the biological scientist.

Conservation

You may want to consider the possibility of becoming a forest ranger or range manager. Much of the United States is forest or rangeland. A forester's chief obligations are to prevent fires and to be generally responsible for the proper maintenance of the trees in a forest and the safety of visitors. The forest manager assumes larger responsibilities according to the uses of the forest; that is, whether the forest is used as a wildlife refuge or for the production of lumber. Range managers monitor the relationship between herd and grassland. They decide which animals to graze on a given spread, how many animals it can support, and to how rotate them to keep the grasses viable.

You might also find your calling as another kind of ranger: a park ranger. Park rangers have a unique, three-pronged responsibility: to enforce civil and environmental laws as a sort of backwoods police officer, to act as custodians for the park land, and to educate and provide information to the public.

Agriculture

The integrity of our food supply system depends on more than just farmers and supermarkets. It also requires agronomists, insect-control specialists, entomologists, veterinarians, and other scientists. Agronomists manage soil health, the germination of crops, and pollution's effects on soil and groundwater. The battle to control insects in farming is age-old, and farms need experts with knowledge of the pests common to certain types of crops.

They take crop samples, assess the plants' vulnerabilities, and apply pesticides to minimize the damage. Entomologists, or insect scientists, study the same subject on a broader level; they might look at samples from across a region to determine a particular insect's range and then estimate the risk to crops accordingly. Agricultural scientists work in many aspects of food production and processing; they may test crops for quality and yield or test plants and animals for resistance to insects and disease. Veterinarians work with large animals as well as small. They work for the government, in private practice, or directly for large farms.

Land Planning

Land planners work for governments or as independent consultants to shape proposed land use to fit existing development and find the right balance for public benefit. Land developers work closely with landscape architects to ensure that the land is suitable for the particular project they are planning and that it complies with environmental regulations. Landscape architects are on-site specialists in the analysis of land features, vegetation, and geography for use in the design of projects in forests, parks, and subdivisions and for airports and highways. Landscape architects are employed by local governments, corporations, or engineering firms. Others are self-employed, often as consultants. To become a landscape architect in the United States, in addition to a bachelor's degree, you'll likely need a state license.

The Geosciences

The government, private industry, architectural firms, and oil companies all employ geologists. Geologists are getting more involved in environmental work, including pollution and waste management. A solid background in mathematics and science is necessary whether you decide to work as an engineering geologist, marine geologist, hydrologist, or mineralogist. A bachelor's degree is the minimum requirement, and a master's degree is needed for some positions.

Pollution Control

There will always be garbage, but local governments and private organizations are employing engineers, chemists, toxicologists, inspectors, and analysts to come up with safe ideas for waste management and to try to recover energy and natural resources. Both government and private industry must also comply with a body of regulations enacted to protect the environment. Widespread recycling cuts down somewhat on the flow of waste to landfills, but a growing population and economy and, well, more stuff to buy make it difficult to stem the tide.

Landfills, which have the potential to pollute nearby groundwater, are inherently unpopular (especially when they need to expand), but more dangerous are the sites that contain hazardous waste and that the EPA must monitor to ensure they're properly managed. Waste management engineers study specifications and plans, inspect disposal facilities, recommend the best ways to dispose of garbage, and develop recovery resources programs.

Environmental specialists also manage every step of civic water supplies, from hydrologic engineers who oversee construction of dams and reservoirs to the technicians who test the water supply at treatment plants to ensure it's safe for public consumption.

Finding the Right Job

Terms such as *job hunt* and *job search* imply that finding the right job is a single act performed within a set period of time, after which point you enter work mode and turn thoughts of your career onto autopilot. The truth is, finding the right job is an art that rewards introspection, hard questions, and trial and error. Some people spend a lifetime searching for their ideal work, but by taking some deliberate steps, you can make the process much shorter than that.

Already we've talked of self-examination, of career tests and research. These are all important components, but sometimes there's no substitute for being in the field. As early as you can, take

advantage of part-time jobs or volunteer opportunities to approximate the sort of work you ultimately intend to do. Experimenta-
tion of this sort is invaluable and perfectly acceptable. If you're
making a midlife career transition, the advice still holds true. Better to take a temporary job to hold down the fort than invest substantial time, money, and effort in a new professional endeavor
only to find it isn't all you thought it would be.

The good news is that the outdoor sciences and their related
professions can be very forgiving when it comes to educational
preparation. You can have taken loads of science courses in high
school or very few, attended a specialized private college known
for its science curriculum or an anonymous state university, grad-
uated at the top of your class or been merely a respectable student.
Of course, taking a lot of science early on, attending the best
schools, and posting excellent grades will make your task easier.
But if you apply yourself, are honest about your interests and abilities, and build the necessary credentials, you can carve out the
career niche you want.

An undergraduate biology degree can lead you in a number of
directions, so if you matriculated thinking you wanted to be an
ornithologist but decide herpetology is more your style, you can
regroup and focus more on reptiles in future classes or with a
graduate degree. Other professions are stricter; a veterinarian
really has no choice other than to graduate from vet school, and a
landscape architect should have at least an undergraduate degree
in landscape architecture. If the educational track seems long or
onerous, remember that the reward of finding the right job is well
worth it. As Confucius said twenty-five hundred years ago,
"Choose a job you love, and you will never have to work a day in
your life." So, read on, contemplate the careers in the following
chapters, and follow your passion.

CHAPTER TWO

Bioscience Careers

areers in the biosciences probably have the broadest range of any we'll cover in this book. In its most basic sense, biology is simply the scientific study of life processes, and the knowledge that biology yields is important to governments, private companies, and the common good of all. With such broad applications, biology majors could go on to fill a staggering array of jobs, from clinical research to consulting to public health. Here, however, we'll focus on those jobs that take their holders into the outdoors regularly, if not full-time, and also provide a sense of purpose and connection with the natural world.

As it turns out, the jobs that fit the bill tend to involve monitoring or safeguarding certain living things' relationships with the larger world: in a word, stewardship. As such, they're often kissing cousins to conservation-oriented jobs like forester, park ranger, and range manager, covered in Chapter 3.

Biology Careers

Scientists pursuing careers in biology apply their flair for analysis, critical thinking, and problem solving to all aspects of the living world, often those with which they feel an intrinsic connection. They might decide to focus on plants, choosing a job in botany. They might opt to work with animals, as ornithologists and mammalogists do. But they need not dedicate themselves to either one exclusively. Many fields of biology are interdisciplinary: oceanographers study many facets of marine life, for example, and botanists might also work in ecology or paleontology, depending on their specialty. For the sake of order, we've arranged zoology and ecology careers as separate sections, but they are in fact branches of biology and closely related to the other biology careers covered here.

A career in any of them could take you to wild local enclaves or to the ends of the earth: forests and parks, zoos, agricultural research stations, rehabilitation facilities, fish hatcheries, ocean-going vessels, or even underwater. Let's take a closer look at your options specifically in biology.

Wildlife Biologists

As a wildlife biologist, you would probably work for the government—federal, state, provincial, or local. On the federal level, the primary employers are the U.S. Fish and Wildlife Service (www.fws.gov) and the Canadian Wildlife Service (www.cws-scf .ec.gc.ca). (Also see "Searching for Biology Jobs" later in this chapter for other agencies hiring biologists.) States and provinces have special departments for the conservation of natural resources or environmental quality. Large cities or counties with parks departments may present opportunities, and independent wildlife preservation societies, sanctuaries, rehabilitation centers, and game preserves also employ wildlife biologists.

What do wildlife biologists do? They study habitat, heritage, and the survival needs of birds, animals, and other living organisms. They study the effects of relationships between species and the effects of pollutants and pesticides on those species. Wildlife biologists also keep track of animals, studying their migration habits, locations, and distribution. They have to study animals' diets and where they find their food, investigate how pollution affects their lives, and generally maintain healthy, balanced populations. Wildlife refuge managers are primarily concerned with the protection and preservation of both indigenous and migratory fish and wildlife and for setting policy for fishing and hunting.

To become a wildlife biologist, you need a college degree in biological sciences, including courses in mammalogy, ornithology, animal ecology, and wildlife management. You would also need to complete courses in comparative anatomy, physiology, zoology, ecology, chemistry, physics, and statistics.

Research Biologists

Whenever there is a variation in the natural environment, caused by such things as land development, temperature alterations, or swamp drainage, natural habitats will change. This has an impact on animal and plant life. Environmental impact statements often have to be prepared to determine whether certain development programs should be attempted if animal and plant life will be destroyed or disrupted. Research biologists, the detectives of the natural world, design experiments and analyze data to answer questions about proper management of specific species or about the interaction between multiple species and their links with the habitat.

They might collect samples in the field to gather information about an animal population's size, diet, diseases, movements, mortality rates, or other statistics, depending on the purpose of a study. Populations and diet are two common subjects of study.

Animal Rehabilitators

Sometimes, due to oil spills, land development, highway construction, trapping, hunting, or natural disasters, animals get injured. Birds can't fly; otters can't swim. Animal rehabilitators, the people who help mitigate the consequences, are usually wildlife and fishery biologists who work either at private or public rehabilitation centers. In college, rehabilitators prepare with course work in anatomy and physiology, ecology, mammalogy, ornithology, and animal behavior. Wild animals inevitably are unpredictable, and injured and vulnerable animals are only more so. Treating wounds or cleaning an animal caught up in an environmental disaster, such as an oil spill, must be undertaken with the utmost care. Before you commit to a career, try to volunteer at an animal shelter, veterinary hospital, or rehabilitation facility and work with animals that are under stress, in shock, or injured.

Animal rehabilitators are on the front lines of protection and preservation of wildlife, birds, and fish. With the threat of further water, air, and land pollution, the rehabilitator will be in greater demand. You can find more information on the field from the National Wildlife Rehabilitators Association (www.nwrawildlife .org), the International Wildlife Rehabilitation Council (www .iwrc-online.org), and Fellow Mortals (www.fellowmortals.org). You'll find, variously, career advice, training opportunities, and job listings.

Ornithologists

Ornithologists study birds and may work as teachers, researchers, or outdoor educators. Many experts believe that bird populations are bellwethers for the health of the larger natural world, so ornithologists' work in preservation of habitat and protection of species' survival is crucial to the overall environment. If you are an avid birder, you may have the beginnings of an ornithological career. Any experience with birds is helpful because an ornithologist's work often has to do with observing and marking them. With birding as an avocation, you may want to explore this career by working as a volunteer or seasonal employee at a park, forest, refuge, zoo, or field station.

If you intend to earn a living as a full-time ornithologist, you need at least a bachelor's degree in biology. In college, you should study anatomy, physiology, ecology, genetics, evolution, and statistics. If your program offers a course in ornithology, take it. Colleges and universities don't offer degrees in ornithology; instead, you would study biology, wildlife biology, zoology, or a related field. Earning a master's degree would require another two to three years of course work and the completion of a thesis and a research project, but it will open the door to higher pay and perhaps the chance to conduct more advanced research. For more information on graduate programs, check out the Wilson Ornithological Society's "Guide to Graduate Studies in Ornithology in North America" (www.ummz.umich.edu/birds/wos).

Competition for jobs is tight, but they're out there—it just depends on how you want to apply your education and experience. Employment with federal, state, and provincial governments is common, and ornithologists also work for conservation agencies, timber and agricultural companies, or as freelancers. You could specialize or integrate ornithology into work as a wildlife biologist or as an endangered species specialist. Most ornithologists do not work with birds exclusively, so gaining broader expertise can be immensely helpful. If you want to work outdoors, you'll probably want to work for a governmental agency rather than in a university or museum.

Governmental agencies are involved in the general field of wildlife management, which includes preservation and study of individual birds and also other types of animals. The U.S. Fish and Wildlife Service (USFWS) manages eight hundred bird species on more than five hundred wildlife refuges, where ornithologists serve as vital liaisons between resident bird populations and the human communities linked to them. The USFWS administers research facilities throughout the country, and most national parks also employ ornithologists. Check out your state, provincial, county, and municipal parks and forest systems as well. (For a list of state and provincial ornithological societies with links to their websites, visit www.nmnh.si.edu/BIRDNET/STATE.html.) State conservation agencies need ornithologists, either as part of general wildlife projects or specialized projects on birds. Field ornithologists are needed for state projects involving endangered and threatened species or status surveys.

Marine and Aquatic Biologists

As a biologist, you may decide to work exclusively with organisms found in water rather than those found on land. You would be called a marine or aquatic biologist, and you might study plankton, mussels, and snails, among other organisms. Although some of your work would be done in the laboratory, you would have to collect actual samples from the water in order to study such information as salt content, acidity, and oxygen level. You would work with organisms in rivers, lakes, and oceans and may need to dive into the water to gather needed materials to be analyzed.

Because of these on-site investigations, aquatic biologists are often called on to make recommendations on environmental matters to other environmental specialists. These may include engineers, pest control specialists, and water pollution analysts or inspectors. Marine biologists may also work in conjunction with marine chemists, whose primary task is to study the organic composition of the ocean. They study changing chemical reactions affecting the food chain as well as the amount of carbon dioxide in the water. Marine biologists also investigate how human waste affects sea life. As a marine biologist, you may also work with geologists, engineers, and oceanographers as well as a variety of technicians.

Marine Mammalogists

Marine mammalogists study ocean-dwelling mammals in three orders: the pinnipeds, flipper-limbed carnivores such as sea lions and walruses; cetaceans, which include whales and dolphins; and sirenians, such as manatees. If you would like to work with marine mammals, you may be in for a difficult but rewarding career. Long days at sea, in laboratories, and at the computer, as well as feeding the animals and cleaning up after them, are part of the job. You could be a field biologist, fishery vessel observer, animal-care specialist, trainer, whale watch guide, or conservation worker.

You have a choice of educational paths: anatomy, physiology, ecology, molecular biology, genetics, veterinary medicine, or management. You would have to decide which marine mammals you would like to study and whether you would like to work for government, industry, oceanaria (large saltwater aquariums), or private organizations. If you decided to study a specific species that is only found in a particular place, you may have to relocate.

High school students should prepare with classes in biology, chemistry, physics, math, computer science, and English. You would need a bachelor of science degree in biology, chemistry, physics, geology, or psychology for an entry-level position. A minor in science, computer science, math, statistics, or engineering could help you in pursuing your career. Be sure to continue to develop your oral and written communications skills. Since you may be interested in marine mammals in other parts of the world, learning a second language would also be helpful. The bachelor's degree would allow you to become a field technician, consultant for industry, or animal-care specialist.

You should also consider graduate school if you want to specialize in marine mammal science. Here you can be a little creative. For example, it may be useful to think about a degree in statistics if you want to study population patterns. Or you could study environmental law or engineering, depending on your particular interest. Your master's degree could help you design research projects, supervise field studies, or lead training programs. Your doctorate would qualify you to coordinate government and corporate projects or management of oceanaria.

Whichever path you choose, it is a good idea to acquire some practical experience as a volunteer at a local or government organization. Zoos, museums, and oceanaria may have internships that would give you skills and help you discover whether this is the field for you. Internships also help you establish a network of people who may recommend you for schools or jobs.

Fish Biologists

As part of wildlife management, you might choose to become a fish biologist. You could find jobs in a natural setting, such as a park, forest, or hatchery. A large part of your work might be to preserve fish habitats by testing water for pollutants. You would spend time on a boat, calculating water volume and collecting fish samples and other organic materials. Based on this study, you could then estimate the fish population for any given lake and plan accordingly. Fish biologists are prominent in ongoing efforts to remove or partially dismantle many dams to restore traditional fish habitats and rehabilitate populations, particularly in the West and particularly with salmon.

To become a fishery biologist, you need a college degree in biology with courses in limnology, fishery biology, aquatic botany, aquatic fauna, oceanography, fish culture, or related courses. Other required courses include general zoology, vertebrate biology, comparative anatomy, and physiology.

Oceanographers

The word *oceanographer* applies to ocean scientists, engineers, and technicians who investigate how the ocean works. Knowledge of the oceans is important for weather and climate information, defense and transportation purposes, and for the study of new food and drug sources. Oceanographers have the power to improve the use of water sources to promote healthy conditions for the species that depend on them.

Physical oceanographers specialize in ocean currents, how they are formed, and what energizes them. While they study light, radar, heat, sound, and wind, their main interests lie in the interaction between the ocean and atmosphere, sea, weather, and climate. Chemical oceanographers concern themselves with chemical compounds and their interactions and with the impact of natural and man-made materials on ocean chemistry. Biological oceanographers explore the interrelationships of oceanic life forms and energy sources, including human impacts.

Geological and geophysical oceanographers study the sediments and rocks on the sea floor. Their observations concern the movement of suspended sediment, the movement of materials on the sea floor, and biological and chemical interactions. Although most oceanographers are basic scientists, they can also be mathematicians or meteorologists. Ocean technicians, who calibrate equipment, take measurements and samples, and repair and maintain instruments are also vital to oceanography.

A degree in oceanography will include the study of physics, chemistry, biology, and geology. Ocean studies tend to be interdisciplinary, though specialties do exist. Oceanography, itself, is a very specialized field and requires at least a bachelor's degree. To pursue a career in ocean science, you'll need a master's degree and, in some cases, a doctorate. If you are in college and preparing to be an oceanographer, you have some serious study ahead of you. Physics, chemistry, biology, geology, geophysics, and even meteorology, math, and engineering are courses you should consider. Good communications skills, a passion for your work, and a considerable talent for science should land you a lasting career in oceanography.

Many universities offer individual courses in the relevant subjects, including graduate programs in oceanography. Visit www.gradschools.com to search for oceanography programs.

Botanists

Botanists specialize in the biology of plants and can work in conservation, natural resources management, agriculture, forestry, horticulture, medicine, or biotechnology. As a botanist, you may further specialize. Plant physiologists study the chemistry and inner workings of plants. Plant ecologists study plants in their natural environments. Pathologists study plant diseases, and taxonomists study plant diversity and classification. Agronomists specialize in farm crops and grasses. You may work in laboratories or in the field, alone or with other scientists. Some of the other areas you could be involved in are biochemistry, ecology, paleobotany (the study of fossilized plants), and genetics.

Zoological Careers

At one time, zoos were more for entertainment and curiosity than for important scientific endeavor. Today they're still fun, but zoos allow us to study animal behavior, illnesses, and physiology while cushioning the blow from habitat loss and attempting to turn the tide with breeding programs. They also help educate the general public about these animals to raise awareness of environmental threats and foster a greater appreciation for wildlife's place in the world. The lofty goals of modern zoos present exciting opportunities for their staffs. Typically, today's zoo has a bird house, a monkey house, and a great ape house. There are elaborate habitats for hoofed animals, elephants, giraffes, lions, tigers, sea lions, beavers, bears, and otters. Amphibians, reptiles, birds, and invertebrates dwell in their own sections. Most zoos also have educational and ecological exhibits and research and breeding facilities. Much of the work at zoological parks is done outside with the animals and is in fact interdisciplinary. Biologists, botanists, ecologists, ornithologists, mammalogists, physiologists, and zoologists work together to try to create environments that approximate those that we have almost destroyed.

Zoologists

Those who wish to work for the conservation, protection, and preservation of individual animals and whole species may choose to become zoologists. The zoologist has the responsibility of planning the collection of animals, maintaining records, and obtaining necessary permits and licenses. Research zoologists are more involved with the ecology and behavior of the animals and seek ways to improve their care. Research may also involve reproduction and breeding in captivity.

Since zoologists study the structures, ecology, functions, and habitats of animals, their knowledge can be applied to wildlife management, conservation, medicine, and agriculture. As a zoologist, you may specialize in ecology, mammalogy, ornithology, entomology (study of insects), ichthyology (study of fish), herpetology (study of reptiles), or ethology (study of animal behavior).

You may be called on to design programs to increase the population of endangered wild or captive animals or to prepare wildlife awareness programs for the general public. As a zoologist, you must be observant, logical, and a team worker.

You don't have to be confined to working in a zoo if you decide to become a zoologist. Aside from state and provincial refuges and preserves, federal wildlife management and conservation agencies such as the U.S. Fish and Wildlife Service, the U.S. Forest Service, the U.S. Bureau of Land Management, and Environment Canada have jobs for zoologists.

Zookeepers

Zookeepers work closely with animals on a daily basis. They feed and water the animals in their care, keep the enclosures clean, and administer medicine under a veterinarian's supervision. They often have to transport animals, keep records on their behavior, and communicate with the public about a variety of species. The zookeeper may specialize in infants or mothers of the newborn or a specific species.

In addition to a love of animals, you need to earn a bachelor's degree in animal behavior, animal science, conservation biology, marine biology, wildlife, or zoology to become a zookeeper. The American Association of Zoo Keepers (AAZK; www.aazk.org) sets standards for animal-care workers in the United States and Canada. It holds conferences, and specific chapters sponsor activities that promote networking. Both the AAZK and the Association of Zoos & Aquariums (www.aza.org) offer job listings on their websites.

Other Zoological Positions

If you chose to work in a zoological park, you could work as a coordinator of volunteers, veterinary technician, gardener, tree worker, or maintenance worker. Many of these are outside jobs that are also needed in parks, science centers, and aquariums.

....

Ecological Careers

Of all the careers we have looked at so far, the ecologist's most thoroughly brings together the study of natural systems—earth, air, water, plants, and animals. Connections between living organisms and the effects of their interactions are the ecologist's concerns. Much of an ecologist's work is done alone, outside—on the ocean, in a rain forest, or in urban settings. That means that ecologists work in all climates throughout the year. They may then be called upon to work in the laboratory to analyze data and write reports and recommendations based on their study. In essence, they investigate and draw conclusions about the balance of nature wherever they find it.

Plant Ecologists

Plant ecologists apply many of the same principles to plant life and study those factors—such as temperature, rainfall, soil content, and elevation—that affect the plant's life cycles. The reproductive life of plants as well as their population patterns and economic worth are part of the plant ecologist's job. As a plant ecologist, you would be working with other professionals whose careers depend on an understanding of plants, such as agricultural scientists, foresters, range managers, and horticulturists.

Animal Ecologists

If you prefer to build your career around the interactions of animals with their environments, you will want to explore the field of animal ecology. These ecologists study not only the present status of animals and their environments but also their origin and history. The study of habitat and diseases as well as the particular geographical location is also a part of the work of the animal ecologist.

Animal ecologists also try to prevent animal extinction by studying, for example, the effects of pesticides on animal populations. Pesticides that are harmful to animals often have the same effects on humans, so this research may also be very helpful to both human and plant life.

Next Steps on the Career Track

Now, how do you get into this field? Top-level high school science courses are a good start. Those already in the field recommend taking advanced biology, chemistry, and physics, as well as math, English, and computer science. It's a good idea to decide on a career path that appeals to you while in high school and choose a college that will help you down that path. High school is also a fine time to look at all aspects of the profession—environment, work hours and schedule, salary, likely job locations, and types of employers—before you commit to a rigorous course of study.

Because of our highly technological society, the applicant with the highest degree of education will probably get the best job. However, a high school diploma could get you a job as a greenhouse aide, animal-care assistant, landscape gardener, or tree worker. With two years of college or some technical training, you could become a technician or warden. Biologists, botanists, zoologists, biotechnologists, and ecologists should have at least a bachelor's degree. For some careers, a master's degree or doctorate is essential.

It is important to recognize that you may be called on to write reports and recommendations, to work with others on team projects, and occasionally to communicate directly with the public—work that will have you behind a desk or otherwise indoors. For example, you may be asked to testify at public hearings based on your knowledge or fieldwork. A well-rounded education will prepare you for all of these eventualities and provide expanded opportunities for advancement.

Job openings in the biological sciences will remain steady in the midterm, growing modestly but amidst increasing competition for openings and research grants. The "romance" of work in marine biology, zoology, and botany will ensure that the number of qualified applicants in those fields continues to far outstrip the available jobs, but dedicated job seekers shouldn't let that dissuade them from their true passion. Perhaps the fastest-growing market for biology majors is in biotechnology, as breakthroughs in manipulation of genes, development of prescription drugs, and sustainable energy production stimulate demand. Not coincidentally, these jobs will also command the highest salaries. The median salary for biotechnology research scientists in 2004 was $62,500, compared with $50,000 for the biological sciences overall. Biotech growth is easily in the double digits over the next ten years, but the prospects for biotech-driven outdoor careers are limited. Variations in salary often have more to do with the level of education, the employer, and your experience than they do your particular specialty.

Searching for Biology Jobs

Because bioscientists are usually part of large institutional infrastructures, such as governments or universities, job searching is relatively straightforward. You can even sift through listings now for jobs you'd like to have several years down the road to see what kinds of experience and education they require and what opportunities they'll present.

The U.S. Government

The Office of Personnel Management (OPM; www.usajobs.gov) is the clearinghouse for nearly all federal jobs in the United States. Using the site, you can search vacancies, sign up for e-mail alerts, create a resume, and apply for specific positions. Applicants must either submit a resume or complete the OF-612 form (www .federaljobs.net/of612.txt). Job hunters applying to the U.S. Fish and Wildlife Service, the largest source of federal government jobs for bioscientists, can also use the Conservation Application Referral Evaluation System (CARES; http://jobsearch.usajobs.opm.gov/a9fws.asp), an integrated part of the USA Jobs system, to search specifically for those positions.

Those looking for thorough coverage of the educational requirements and skills necessary for government hiring in given fields can consult the *Qualifications Standards for General Schedule Positions* (www.opm.gov/qualifications). The guide spells out policies, career tracks, and specialized experience for all types of government jobs, but it's intended as a broad overview; the best information about specific openings is in the listings themselves.

General Schedule (GS) refers to the employment level, a number assigned to all federal government hires and one that changes as the employee advances. You'll see the codes, which range from GS-1 to GS-15, in listings for every civil service position; each level has its own salary range and educational standards. Within each GS level, there are ten sublevels, so a job posting might identify an opening as "GS-0607," meaning GS-6, sublevel 7. Higher education and more experience generally qualify you for a higher GS level, which also means a higher salary. The federal government grants preferences to veterans, sometimes waiving requirements. Note that when many candidates apply for the same job, the agency suspends the registration process so that no new applicants can apply.

In the United States, numerous departments and agencies hire scientists for work in the outdoors:

Department of the Interior
- U.S. Fish and Wildlife Service
- Bureau of Land Management
- National Park Service
- U.S. Geological Survey

Department of Agriculture
- Forest Service
- Natural Resources Conservation Service
- Animal and Plant Health Inspection Service

Environmental Protection Agency

Department of Commerce
- National Oceanic and Atmospheric Administration

The Canadian Government

Most civil hiring for the Canadian government goes through the Public Service Commission of Canada (www.jobs-emplois.gc.ca). Check out the Public Service Commission's guide to applying for jobs with the Canadian government (www.jobs-emplois.gc.ca/menu/job_guide_e.htm). The setup and application process is much the same as for U.S. jobs. Job postings can change quickly; some are open for as little as forty-eight hours. To ensure you don't miss an opportunity, you can check for jobs frequently or request that the Public Service Commission e-mail you about openings that fit your interests and qualifications. You do not necessarily need to be a Canadian citizen to obtain most government jobs in Canada, but you must at least be a permanent resident or hold a special status that allows you to work in the country. Hiring agencies do generally give preference to Canadian citizens.

The Treasury Board of Canada's collective agreements with assorted professional and labor unions govern salaries and work conditions for government positions. Biologists, foresters, and agricultural workers are bound by agreements made with the Professional Institute of the Public Service of Canada (www.pipsc.ca), which represents nearly fifty thousand federal, provincial, and territorial government employees. Classifications and subclassifications depend on the area of employment, but current pay rates for various employment levels are available at www.tbs-sct.gc.ca/hr-rh/lr_ca_rp-rt_cc_tr/index_e.asp. (Click on "Rates of Pay for the Public Service of Canada." The abbreviation for biological scientists is "BI.")

Hiring agencies in the Canadian government include:

Environment Canada
- Canadian Wildlife Service
- Parks Canada
- Canadian Environmental Assessment Agency

Natural Resources Canada
- Canadian Forest Service

Fisheries and Oceans Canada
- Fisheries Research Conservation Council

Jobs with States and Provinces

Although federal governments are major employers of environmental workers, you will also find jobs at the state or provincial, county, and municipal levels of government. Many states and provinces have rather stringent requirements for employment, including physical health, education, and experience. Be sure to check with the agency for all those details before you apply. Government jobs are fairly stable, and the career track is clearly spelled out for you. On the other hand, they are also very competitive, so education and training are paramount.

Each state has a slightly different name for its conservation or wildlife agency: the Department of Fish and Game, Division of Fisheries and Wildlife, Department of Natural Resources, or Environmental Conservation Division. For links to individual state conservation departments, visit www.fws.gov/offices/statelinks .html. For provincial conservation sites, visit the Canadian Wildlife Service's link page at www.cws-scf.ec.gc.ca/other_e.cfm. Earnings at the state and provincial level are somewhat lower than at the federal level. In the United States, state-level biologists averaged about $43,500 in 2004, compared with $47,000 at the federal level. In Canada, the average in the provinces worked out to Can$48,000 for 2004. In 2005 U.S. employees with bachelor's degrees in biology started at about $31,000.

Jobs in the Private Sector

This is a growing area for jobs in the biosciences. As the trend toward outsourcing of government work continues, biologists will find more opportunities with private companies. Most jobs will remain in the public sector, but major corporations and specific industries, such as extraction, timber, and agricultural sectors, also have substantial environmental obligations and regulations to follow and therefore hire biologists to help them comply.

There are three main areas in the private sector for work:

- corporations
- private universities
- nonprofit environmental organizations

Pay is generally best with corporations, followed by universities and then nonprofits, but the responsibilities and specialties are so diverse that average numbers don't mean much. The approach to the job search is different here. There is no one source with information on all the openings you might be qualified for, so you'll need to cast your net wider. Let friends, family, and people you've met in the field know what type of job you're looking for and where you want to work. Check out science career–oriented websites such as www.biologyjobs.com and the American Institute of Biological Sciences (www.aibs.org/classifieds) for openings and mainstream catch-all job boards such as Monster (www .monster.com) and Yahoo! HotJobs (www.hotjobs.yahoo.com). For university jobs, check the sites of individual colleges and universities, which frequently post their open positions online, and the *Chronicle of Higher Education* (www.chronicle.com) for leads. This book's Appendix includes information on a number of professional associations with job boards and also lists other job-hunting sites.

Nonprofits hire biologists on a much smaller scale and might have limited funds to compete on the salary front. Nonetheless, many find the work immensely rewarding and the colleagues inspirational. The larger organizations include Greenpeace (www.greenpeace.org), the Sierra Club (www.sierraclub.org), and the Nature Conservancy (www.nature.org).

CHAPTER THREE

Conservation Careers

A ll the careers in this book involve stewardship of the natural world in some way, but the tracks in Chapter 3 deal directly with the land: wild forests and open range. These are the places that make all the fauna possible—you can't save an animal species without preserving the ecosystem in which it thrives. The conservation of natural resources is a multidimensional and integrated search for solutions to the challenges of stewardship. So, a forester or a range manager incorporates many of the same principles and training into his or her work that an ecologist or wildlife biologist might.

Managing Our Forests

Forests, with their complex ecosystems and valuable timber, symbolize the sometimes thin line between conservation and exploitation. Is the forest being managed for the health of its trees and the wildlife it sustains or for commercial interests? The two are not incompatible, but with so many biological variables and competing human interests, people are bound to disagree.

The USDA Forest Service (www.fs.fed.us) manages 193 million acres of forest land, and there are 750 million total acres of forest land in the United States (and 766 million in Canada), so many people with diverse skills are needed to make sure that our forests are well maintained. Different types of forests include municipal, county, community, and federal parks; rangelands and wildlife sanctuaries; swampland; watersheds; and timberland and wilderness areas. Some of these areas are used for recreation, others for habitat restoration. Some are used for logging, others for wildlife protection. And some are used for cattle grazing, others for animal rehabilitation.

Both independent and government organizations and agencies are working, sometimes together, sometimes at odds with each other, to effectively manage, preserve, and restore the land and its resources. Private, state, provincial, and national forests may serve several purposes—recreational, industrial, and environmental—and sometimes these purposes do not coincide. For example, the paper industry needs wood from the trees in the forest, but trees remove carbon dioxide from the air and help offset global warming, as illustrated by the difference in carbon dioxide levels between winter and summer in the northern hemisphere, which has a much larger land mass and therefore many more trees than the southern hemisphere. (Winter levels are significantly higher.) Trees are also natural habitats for various species of wildlife and birds. So, conflicts arise between the human need for employment, paper, and construction materials that the logging industry provides and the growing awareness among private citizen groups of the importance of preserving the balance of nature.

Some of the hottest disputes have arisen over how to manage fire on public lands; what constitutes "salvage" timber; whether the most remote sections of national forests should be off-limits to the construction of additional logging roads, which make those areas ineligible for wilderness designation; and management of Alaska's Tongass National Forest, the world's largest temperate coastal rainforest and repository of huge tracts of old-growth forest, for nakedly commercial interests.

The timber and energy-development companies profiting from federal contracts routinely square off against the independent environmental groups that carefully monitor habitat destruction, endangerment of species, and waste of resources. When governmental agencies that are charged with stewardship of public lands engage in practices that will adversely affect the life of various species in parks or forests, environmentally oriented organizations protest the action. When land developers or oil companies threaten animal or plant habitats, they can also expect vociferous protest from these same organizations.

Much research and effort, for example, has gone into preservation of tropical rain forests and economic programs that allow their residents to prosper without degrading vital ecosystems. Many companies have pledged to refrain from buying products originating in endangered rainforests or produced on recently deforested rainforest land, such as beef. Widespread recycling programs are redirecting some of our waste from landfills, though not enough, and furnishing consumers with a steady supply of recycled paper products.

Forestry Careers

Passions run high when it comes to natural resource management and preservation, especially considering how many millions of acres are involved. And when you choose a career in conservation of parks or forests, you should think about whether you want to work for a governmental agency that has to follow the policy of the current administration or for an independent, grassroots organization that targets a specific species or devotes itself to playing the watchdog role for a variety of environmental issues. Whichever path you choose, commitment, education, endurance, skill, creativity, training, knowledge of the law, and sometimes physical strength will determine your career path.

Federal Government Jobs in Forestry

The Forest Service, part of the U.S. Department of Agriculture, employs about thirty thousand permanent employees and fifteen thousand temporary employees. Among these are several thousand foresters and forest technicians. The number of staff positions with the Forest Service changes with the political environment. In the 1960s and 1970s, the service created many new positions, including wildlife biologist, landscape architect, land management planner, and soil conservationist. In the 1980s and early 1990s, it expanded further by adding positions in law enforcement, recreation, planning, and conservation. In the past decade, it has deemphasized its timber sale program and reduced its workforce by outsourcing jobs as much as possible. The shift has left fieldworkers with more paperwork as they cover the loss of administrative staff and cope with having fewer foresters overall. Though the government will continue to hire foresters and forest technicians, this job market will decline somewhat for the foreseeable future.

The research branch of the Forest Service employs more than twenty thousand people. Its research scientists work in universities, laboratories, and stations all over the United States and study tree improvement; forest protection from fire, diseases, and pests; wilderness management; forest engineering; and urban forestry, among others.

The Canadian Forest Service (www.cfs.nrcan.gc.ca), part of Natural Resources Canada, is the federal-level department charged with managing Canada's forest resources. Canada generally has a progressive outlook on forest management, seeking to balance sustainability with a thriving logging industry, and with 10 percent of the world's forests, it's no small feat. Yet the regulatory duties are much more decentralized in Canada than in the United States. The provinces and territories own three-quarters of the country's forests and handle management of those lands and related legislation.

Foresters

Forests are probably best known for trees, but they also provide recreational opportunities and wildlife habitat. So foresters manage these areas in a variety of ways. In private lands, they may deal more with negotiating timber sales by working with loggers and pulpwood cutters. They have to balance the economic and recreational purposes with the environmental impact on ecosystems within the forest. They have to determine how to preserve habitats, water quality, and soil stability in order to conform to environmental standards and regulations. Among the duties of the forester in the state, provincial, or federal systems are the management of public forests, campgrounds, and other recreational areas.

If lumber is a major product of a particular forest, foresters have to know the size of the trees and how much lumber the trees can yield. When foresters decide which trees are to be cut, they also have to decide which trees will replace them. If there is a forest fire, it may be necessary to replace a large section of the forest.

As a forester, you may also be able to choose a specialty, such as research, fire prevention, disease control, soil erosion, or logging practices. In addition to very specific knowledge about forest ecology, foresters have to supervise and train other workers, know all the laws and enforce them, travel when necessary, and react quickly to emergencies.

You would need a bachelor's degree in forestry and some practical experience to become a forester. Participation in field trips or camps sponsored by forestry schools would give you a feel for this type of work. Or you could use your summer breaks to work in a city, state, or provincial park or forest, or you could volunteer with a grassroots environmental group. Some colleges may accept this work for credit.

In addition to your forestry courses, you must have highly developed oral and written communication skills as well as mathematics, biometrics, and computer knowledge. If you choose to specialize in a particular field or to engage in research, you would need an advanced degree. Specialties include wildlife conservation, entomology, genetics, tree culture, wood technology, and recreation. Median annual earnings for U.S. foresters in 2004 were $48,000.

Finding a Job

Other federal agencies employing foresters are the Bureau of Land Management (www.blm.gov), the National Park Service (www.nps.gov), the Bureau of Indian Affairs (www.doi.gov/bureau-indian-affairs.html), and the Tennessee Valley Authority (www.tva.gov), the nation's largest public power company. Every state has some agency concerned with forests, parks, and conservation that provides career opportunities for foresters. Urban forestry, which involves tree care in city parks and streets—and the stresses and challenges endemic to urban environments (think utility poles and power lines)—continues to grow, and private consulting firms as well as grassroots environmental groups hire foresters.

The Society of American Foresters (www.safnet.org) is a professional scientific and educational organization that advocates professional forest management with certification programs for foresters and forest technicians. Its website provides information about forestry careers, resources for professionals, and a career center with job listings and tools for job seekers.

The Canadian Forest Service has much the same mission as the USDA Forest Service, and Parks Canada correlates to the National Park Service in the United States. Find out about available jobs at the Canadian Forest Service through Natural Resources Canada (www.nrcan.gc.ca/careers/eng/apply-e.htm) and Parks Canada (www.pc.gc.ca/agen/empl/index_e.asp). The Canadian Institute of Forestry (www.cif-ifc.org) also works for the proper stewardship of Canadian forests by setting professional standards; holding national conferences; and conducting field trips, scientific presentations, and public speaking engagements. It has approximately twenty-seven hundred members in eighteen sections in Canada, and its members include scientists, foresters, technicians, and technologists.

As you can see, though not a dynamic growth area, opportunities for foresters exist in national, state, provincial, and private forests and in cities, industry, and independent organizations. You may choose to become a forest technician or work in a nursery for a while before committing to the additional educational requirements of foresters.

Forest Technicians

The forest technician's work in forests and parks is vital to the proper use of the land. Much of the work has to do with patrolling the land, preserving it from ravaging fires, and protecting trees and the life forms dependent on them.

As a forest technician, you would be called on to assist foresters in planting trees, preventing fires, and constructing roads. One type of technician is the surveyor, who maps out where roads will be built. Other technicians are responsible for the health of the trees, so they inspect for harmful insects and diseases; prune or destroy trees when necessary; and pollinate, graft, and gather seeds under the supervision of the forester or plant scientist.

You may need supervisory skills if you oversee work crews for road building and repair, planting trees, and fighting fires. Map interpretation, data collecting, and report writing might be part of the job. Many tools are required to keep parks and forests in good condition, and you may have to use and repair them. You may also have to maintain buildings, do carpentry work, and purchase provisions for work crews.

The work changes with the seasons. Planting is carried out at certain times, harvesting at others. Most of your work would be outdoors, and you may have to live in the park or forest where you work. You would also need to be ready to handle emergencies in any area of the park, no matter what the weather conditions are. Because technicians often must travel long distances in a large park or forest, you should have physical stamina. You would often have to walk on rugged terrain while carrying heavy supplies. Or you may have to ride a horse or travel in a helicopter to cover all the territory in a jurisdiction.

To become a forest technician requires at least a high school diploma. Your diploma may be from a vocational high school, but your studies should include plenty of math and science. Since you may have to communicate with the public and write reports, you should have solid communication skills, too. After high school, you should gain at least two years of experience in forestry, either through an associate's degree or time on the job. Valuable work experience could include farming, logging, surveying, or construction. You would also need a license to drive trucks and perhaps farm equipment, such as tractors.

During your summer vacations, you may want to work in a local park or forest, state conservation bureau, or with the USDA Forest Service or Canadian Forest Service. The Bureau of Land Management may also have summer jobs available. The National Park Service offers a Volunteers in the Parks program (www.nps.gov/volunteer) for those who wish to try their hand at this work before committing to an actual career. Some community and vocational schools offer two-year degrees in general forestry, wildlife conservation, and forest harvesting. If you combined these courses with fieldwork where you have the opportunity to observe forest workers, you would be in a better position to find a job as a forest technician.

Technicians in parks and forests may have a choice of seasonal or temporary work. Also, work is centered in the heavily forested parts of the country, of course. With your high school diploma and two years of additional schooling, on-the-job experience may put you in line for more responsibilities. But you would need more education if you wanted to become a forester or park ranger.

As noted earlier, government work in forestry is something of a declining field, which is not to say there aren't jobs available. But work with private companies, such as in consulting, is where the market is expanding. And you would probably make more money working for private industry than for government. Entry-level salaries vary with experience and training, but the median wage for U.S. forest technicians in 2004 was about $13.14 per hour.

. . . .

Parks Careers

The National Park Service (NPS) employs more than twenty thousand permanent and temporary workers and 125,000 volunteers. Its mission is to manage and protect almost four hundred natural, cultural, and recreational areas. Its headquarters is in Washington, D.C., with seven regional offices (Alaska Area, Intermountain, Midwest, National Capital, Northeast, Pacific West, and Southeast), an interpretive design center, and a service center. The NPS has sites in the United States, Guam, Puerto Rico, and the Virgin Islands. Temporary jobs are very competitive. Internships are available, and interns are hired by individual parks, so you should determine where you want to work and apply directly. The Student Conservation Association (www.thesca.org) administers three volunteer and internship programs with stints ranging from three weeks to a year. Resource assistants work for the NPS and other federal agencies. If you're interested in a career or a seasonal job with the NPS, you can search for job openings and apply online through the U.S. Office of Personnel Management (www.usajobs.opm.gov).

Parks Canada (www.pc.gc.ca) manages thirty-nine national parks, including such jewels as Banff, Kluane, and Forillon, and some of the wildest and most pristine territory in the world. Duties with Parks Canada are much the same as with the NPS. The agency employs four thousand (seven thousand during the summer), including more than four hundred park wardens (the equivalent to park rangers in Canada). The parks also hire cultural interpreters, archaeologists, tradespeople, and historians. Search for openings and apply online at www.jobbank.gc.ca.

Park Rangers

At the heart of the NPS are the park rangers, whose primary responsibilities include management of wildlife, lakeshores, seashores, and recreation areas. When you first start out, you may be assigned to operate campgrounds by supplying firewood, assigning campsites, and providing security. Or you may be employed in a city or rural park, and most of your work will be done outdoors.

Much of your work would involve patrolling the park to prevent unlawful hunting, enforce regulations, inspect trees for disease, and report dangerous situations and emergencies to the park supervisor. Some of your work would also be educating the public on natural and historical features, giving informational speeches, and assisting with research projects.

Park rangers instruct the public on safety procedures for water sports, prevention of fires and accidents, and administering first aid. So you'd have to develop good communication skills for educational purposes and also to settle disputes or clear up misunderstandings among park users.

Park rangers should have at least two years of college with a minimum of twelve credits in science and criminal justice. Courses in natural resource management, natural or earth sciences, park and recreation management, archaeology, and anthropology are very helpful. Rangers also receive on-the-job training that is often supplemented with more formal training sessions. Six-month training programs are available at Grand Canyon National Park in Arizona and at Harpers Ferry, West Virginia. The possibility for promotion would be to district ranger, park manager, or staff specialist. Further education may be required for these promotions. Jobs with the service are competitive, and park budgets appear tighter than ever. Political tides might well determine the future market for park service personnel. Summer rangers with a college degree start at just under $19,000 annualized. Full-time rangers with degrees started between $21,000 and $32,000 in 2005. In Canada, park wardens started at Can$25,000 for seasonal work, and full-time wardens earned between Can$45,000 and Can$60,000 in 2005.

Range Management Careers

Managing grazing land for both livestock and wildlife also offers opportunities for employment for nature lovers who want to work outdoors. This land is called the range, and it also needs managers or conservationists. Often these lands are used for recreation and as natural habitats for animals.

Range Managers

As a range manager, you would decide which animals would graze on the land and select the proper grazing seasons. Sometimes you would work as a combination forester, wildlife conservationist, soil erosion specialist, and habitat rehabilitator. To handle the duties, you need to know about vegetation, watershed processes, farming, and ecological interrelationships. To become a range manager, you need a bachelor's degree in that field. Your course work might include biology, chemistry, physics, plant and animal physiology, and soil sciences. Good communications and computer skills as well as courses in wildlife and forestry are helpful.

Because most rangeland is in the West, you may have to relocate to find employment as a range manager. Jobs in the United States are available through the USDA Forest Service and Bureau of Land Management, in Canada through the Canadian Forest Service and Natural Resources Canada. State and provincial conservation agencies provide additional career opportunities. You can also find employment on privately owned ranches or at universities doing research. Median salary for U.S. range managers in 2004 was $52,000.

As with any career, it is a good idea to become affiliated with a professional organization. The Society for Range Management (www.rangelands.org) is a professional scientific and conservation organization whose mission is "to promote the professional development and continuing education of members and the public and the stewardship of rangeland resources." It publishes a bimonthly magazine of science and range news called *Rangelands,* and land managers, conservationists, scientists, and educators from the United States, Canada, and abroad are among its four thousand members.

The Battle for Land Use

Protecting the wildlife, fish, birds, and trees on the nation's many acres of public and private land requires a wide variety of professionals with a deep commitment to all species affected by change created by humans. One of the struggles over public lands today is going on between land developers and environmentalists. Developers make their living by building new structures that fill some human need, whether recreational or commercial. Many believe that human needs supersede the needs of all other species. Environmentalists are generally not in accord with this belief, and that is where conflicts arise.

The approach to solving such problems is becoming more and more holistic or integrated, with many committed professionals trying to preserve all species in healthy and nurturing habitats. When we lose a species, we know that we will never be able to retrieve it—it is gone forever. It has already happened to many species. Others are barely hanging on to existence, often in unnatural environments.

Ongoing research is giving us a better picture of daily movements and migration patterns of numerous species, and in turn the amount of a given habitat they need to reasonably survive. Habitats everywhere are being carved up by new and expanded roads, developments, and energy exploration. To offset the effects of this relentless march, ecologists and wildlife managers are emphasizing "greenways," intact corridors that permit animals to pass from one tract to another, sometimes over or under interstates, and avoid the encroachment of the human world. This is especially important for large, wide-ranging mammals such as bears and wolves, but for many smaller species as well.

Many range managers, wildlife managers, biologists, foresters, and park rangers work to reclaim certain habitats or to prevent further destruction from development. Land planners and landscape architects are also called in to investigate the ecology of an area before developers can build a road, a shopping mall, or a recreational facility. Modern regulations tend to require developers who destroy a wildlife habitat to construct a comparable one—whether or not a species is endangered. In the case of fish, for example, a hatchery may need to be constructed when a river or streambed is dammed.

For this reason, some developers and corporations may hire specialists to restore habitats. These might include wildlife biologists, fish biologists, and culturists. State and provincial governments are also becoming aware of habitat problems as new suburban housing developments encroach on homes of deer, beaver, gophers, and raccoons who forage for food in garbage cans because their natural food supply has been destroyed. Or they may move into the garage, basement, or attic, seeking shelter because the trees and bushes that have protected them are gone.

Many highly skilled professionals and technicians are needed just to meet today's environmental needs. Common species as well as endangered species of animals and plants must be protected, as well as forests, parks, grasslands, and wetlands.

How you want to contribute to the local, state, or federal parks and forests or to private industry or grassroots organizations may depend on how much time you want to devote to education and training and whether you want to specialize in forestry, wildlife biology, ornithology, or fisheries. If you're more comfortable on the ranch or farm, you may want to become a range manager. The future holds many potential changes as land, water, and air continue to be threatened with pollution and development. Increasing regulations and awareness will require many committed professionals seeking to solve complex environmental problems. You may be one of the lucky ones to participate in the process.

CHAPTER FOUR

Agricultural Careers

The purpose of agriculture, the science of producing crops and livestock, is to increase food production and protect the land from deterioration. In its early history, agriculture encouraged stable human settlements and was an economic and social organizational force. During the sixteenth and seventeenth centuries, crop and farming methods became more sophisticated, and in the nineteenth century, the invention of farm machines increased production. Modern agriculture methods involve the use of pesticides and fertilizers, refrigeration, and the creation of genetically engineered food. Agriculture affects all of us because it supplies our food, one of the most fundamental human needs.

Agriculture historically has been a powerful economic and social force in human life. However, the picture of the family farm with a big red barn, animals roaming freely, and acres of verdant crops is mostly a quaint relic of yesteryear. Unstable prices, aided by federal farm policies, favor corporate operations that can cover bad seasons and remain profitable on tremendous volume. In the United States, there are four million fewer family farms now than there were fifty years ago, and the average farmer is nearing retirement age. Family farms have been superseded largely by agribusiness—huge conglomerates condemned by many for confining animals in small, overcrowded cages; using antibiotics and growth hormones in livestock and poultry; treating crops with pesticides; and producing genetically modified (GM) and irradiated food.

The changes in the past fifty years are the result of better machinery, the increased sophistication of research techniques, corporate involvement in the food chain, and the availability of rapid global communication and transportation. The changes often have rendered farming highly efficient. At the same time, cutting corners can have social costs measured by risks to public health and the degradation of farms and contiguous land. For example, the incidence in mad cow disease in England triggered a general boycott of beef exports from that country. Given the choice, cattle eat grass and, to a lesser extent, grain. They are herbivores by nature. But England produces little soy, the protein supplement popular with most North American producers to improve weight gain, so its cattle were fed a blend of meat and bone meal made from slaughterhouse scraps and the ground-up carcasses of other cattle, many of which it can be assumed were sick or otherwise unfit for slaughter. Combined with the relaxing of British laws to allow sterilization of the rendered meal at lower temperatures—again, to cut costs—cattle in England were more likely to suffer from mad cow (bovine spongiform encephalopathy) than cattle elsewhere in Europe.

Similarly, scattered outbreaks of the *E. coli* virus in contaminated meat and produce and the perpetuation of other pathogens in the food supply through negligence of safeguards have made people more cautious about conventionally grown and processed foods. Organically grown and processed meat, eggs, dairy products, fruits, and vegetables are becoming more popular every day.

All of these issues are part of an international concern for the health and safety of the food we eat. People all over the world are more aware of the origins of the food they consume. International trade agreements involving food are often challenged because of varying food policies in each country.

Some people favor abolishing genetically modified food; others want it labeled so that the consumer can make the choice. The United States leads the world in the amount of GM crops grown, and many other countries are steadily increasing their already significant share of those crops, including Argentina, Canada, Brazil, and China. In the United States, soybeans lead the way in terms of acreage dedicated to GM crops, with nearly 90 percent of them GM. Cotton and corn also are big: about 75 percent of U.S. cotton is GM, and about half of all U.S. corn, with those percentages on the rise. People worry about these food products introducing contamination to other species. Many GM foods were developed to withstand pesticides, but in the process, some weeds are becoming immune to insecticides. People who are allergic to certain foods may not know whether genes from those foods have been spliced into a food product they are not allergic to.

The U.S. Department of Agriculture (www.usda.gov) and the Food and Drug Administration (www.fda.gov) set regulatory standards for food and drugs in the United States. In Canada, the task falls to Health Canada (www.hc-sc.gc.ca). Since people are now more informed about what is happening in this field, new challenges and opportunities are "on the plate" for these agencies. Because consumers are concerned about pesticides, they have turned in growing numbers to foods labeled organic, and the USDA has set strict standards for what products qualify as organic through its National Organic Program (see www.ams.usda.gov/nop/indexNet.htm). After years of debate, Canada instituted an "Organic Canada" label (see www.pwgsc.gc.ca/cgsb/on_the_net/organic/index-e.html) in 2006 that consolidates into a single standard the slew of unofficial organizational certifications the country's growers had relied on previously.

Careers in Agriculture

Don't be daunted by the challenges that short-sighted business strategies have created for the sustainability of agriculture and, indirectly, all of us. Those problems mean only that the field is in critical need of new ways of thinking and people who can make food production beneficial for producers, consumers, and the environment. As consumers gain more information about how their food is produced, the changes they demand will open new job opportunities to all involved in the food supply chain.

Agronomists

Agronomy goes hand in hand with agriculture because it is concerned with soil management and the breeding, physiology, and production of crops. Major crops, such as cotton, soybeans, and wheat, are its chief concern.

Much of the effort of today's agronomists is applied to reducing environmental pollution. Some agronomists may be primarily concerned with how pesticides react in the soil and groundwater. They investigate how long it takes for them to break down and how toxic the process will be. Others concentrate on the dumping of waste material into the soil. Still other agronomists, who want to work more closely with farming problems, work at agricultural extension services. These are usually located at land-grant universities, where agronomists work with specific problems of farmers and help them to better manage their farms. The U.S. government employs agronomists in the Natural Resources Conservation Service (www.nrcs.usda.gov) and the U.S. Forest Service (www.fs.fed.us). In Canada, look to Agriculture and Agri-Food Canada (www.agr.gc.ca). These agronomists are concerned primarily with farmers and ranchers and how they can manage their land effectively and conserve the soil at the same time. Some agronomists are becoming farmers and ranchers themselves and using their college or university education on their own crops and soil to make a living.

Since agronomists are involved in the vital work of crop production and soil conservation, their work is needed all over the world. Universities, government agencies, and various foundations, as well as agriculture-related businesses with branches in foreign countries, need the services of agronomists to help solve the nutritional needs of developing nations throughout the world. So if you have a bit of wanderlust, you may consider agronomy as a career.

To become an agronomist, start out by studying the basic sciences in high school, including biology, chemistry, math, and physics. English is required, and foreign languages are recommended to interface in a global economy. In college take geology, botany, microbiology, genetics, plant physiology, soil chemistry, plant pathology, entomology, biochemistry, and meteorology. With a bachelor of science degree, you could be a farmer, agricultural agent, or soil conservationist.

If you decide to get a master's degree, you will find more career opportunities available, both in research and agricultural extension programs. Both governmental and private-sector agencies and organizations need highly skilled and educated professionals now and in the future as the need for environmentally safe crops and "clean" soil continues. The median salary for U.S. agronomists in 2004 was $50,000.

Agricultural Pest Control

If you are a nature lover interested in working on agricultural problems but you don't want to devote as much time to your education as an agronomist, you may consider the career of agricultural pest control specialist. On the job, you would take samples of crops and inspect them for signs of dangerous organisms or harmful insect infestation. You would be able to assist in proposing effective methods of disease prevention or using predators to eradicate the offending pests.

The specialist often trains and coordinates crews of workers who are brought in to spray pesticides after they learn to operate the equipment and applicators. At this level, the specialist also has to use management skills to make assignments, train workers, evaluate them, and be responsible for the working order of all equipment. Pest control specialists are responsible for working with farmers and governmental agencies. They may work on land or occasionally from airplanes, where they apply pesticides from the air. U.S. pest control workers in 2004 earned a median wage of $12.60 an hour, with certified technicians and supervisors earning more.

To be hired as a trainee, you should have two years of full-time agricultural work experience in such jobs as farm operator, field sweeper, assistant to a specialist, or in a regulatory role with the government. At least one year of that time should be in a capacity other than pesticide operator. As a pest control specialist, you will have to be knowledgeable about surveying and controlling pests as well as about the current laws and regulations regarding pesticides.

Your prospects for employment as a pest control specialist are quite good, primarily with state, provincial, and federal government agencies. Some states now require licensing, so be sure to check with your state's licensing board. In order to issue a license, many states now require you to have a college degree, so you will have to keep up with the changing educational standards for licensing.

For more information on licensing requirements in the United States, visit the Environmental Protection Agency's resource page on state certification programs at www.epa.gov/pesticides/safety/applicators/statepro.htm.

For certification information from Health Canada's Pest Management Regulatory Agency, visit www.pmra-arla.gc.ca/english/fpt/edutran-e.html.

Pest Control Assistants. Those who want to enter the pest control field before committing to a great deal of education should consider starting out as a pest control assistant. As an assistant, you would help control rodents in agricultural fields and buildings. You might set traps, dig out harmful weeds, burn or spray, and try to identify likely places of infestation.

To become a pest control helper, you must be healthy and strong, dexterous and agile. But there are no educational standards or work experience requirements for the job. You may then advance, with some work experience, to a position as a pest exterminator.

Pest Exterminators. Pest exterminators are employed by private industry and are found in the city and on the farm. Pests can infest not only crops but also buildings and other farm facilities and even farm animals. After initial inspections, exterminators make recommendations for treatment. Much of your work as a pest exterminator will be outdoors in all kinds of weather conditions. It will be strenuous and may involve bending, crawling, climbing, and lifting. You will have to be physically strong and have stamina to do this kind of work. Although there are no educational requirements, some states require licensing. You will have to know the rules and regulations concerning pesticides, dangerous pests, and extermination and prevention methods. You generally become an exterminator by receiving on-the-job training as an assistant.

The Pesticide Controversy. The use of pesticides has, of course, caused a great deal of controversy. Many that were used in the past are considered too toxic for use now and have been banned. Some that are now used are being challenged by independent organizations as being carcinogenic or too toxic for use in the food chain. Federal, state, provincial, and local governments have set up regulatory agencies for toxins and pesticides, and private organizations serve a vital watchdog function, helping ensure those agencies are working effectively to protect the environment and plant, animal, and human life.

The United States Federal Insecticide, Fungicide, and Rodenticide Act of 1947 was regularly amended in the 1970s, 1980s, and 1990s. Essentially, it provides for federal control over the application of pesticides and regulation of the marketing of these products. The legislation underscores the fact that protection of the environment is everybody's job and that particular attention has to be paid to any substance used on crops or in the soil that holds the crops. For instance, a U.S. Geological Survey study found that pesticides commonly used on crops in Illinois were getting into the rainwater by evaporating into the clouds. As these clouds moved, the polluted rain could then fall in any location. The pesticides in question were atrazine, alachlor, and metolachlor. In some places where the rainwater had fallen, the concentration of pesticides exceeded the U.S. Environmental Protection Agency (EPA) standards. This may be why traces of the now-banned DDT can still be found all over the world. It also demonstrates that environmental concerns are global and must be tackled both locally and globally. Government, industry, and private associations must continually monitor the natural environment and make their reports known to the public for its input.

The EPA acknowledges that the use of pesticides is a two-edged sword. Some pesticides have actually reduced crop damage; others have saved lives by controlling insects that carry diseases. They have helped to preserve forests and parks and have stopped fruit from dropping before it is ripe. They can also retard fungicidal growth.

But whenever they stay in the environment and spread beyond the intended area, they may invade the food we eat, the air we breathe, and the land that sustains the food. They become dangerous and harmful. They may even affect the reproductive cycle of certain birds and the ability of species to survive.

Finding ways to reduce the use of pesticides harmful to humans and the natural environment is increasingly important. As our population grows, protecting our groundwater from contamination by pesticides and reducing the impacts on wildlife already suffering habitat loss will be paramount. In the United States, the federal agencies responsible for monitoring toxic substances are the EPA (www.epa.gov), the Food and Drug Administration (www.fda.gov), the Occupational Health and Safety Administration (www.osha.gov), and the Consumer Product Safety Commission (www.cpsc.gov). The EPA is primarily responsible for the protection of the environment from pesticides. In Canada it's the Pest Management Regulatory Agency (www.pmra-arla.gc.ca), a division of Health Canada, and the Commercial Chemicals Division of Environment Canada (www.ec.gc.ca/NOPP/ccd/en/index .cfm?par_OrgID=5&par_Org=1).

Entomologists

Entomologists are divided into two categories: systematic and economic. Both work with insects. Systematic entomologists work in laboratories; economic, in the field. Economic entomologists determine the geographic range of insects through surveys and then evaluate their economic impact.

You can become an entomologist with a bachelor's degree with emphasis on entomology and the zoological sciences. You must know how to classify major pests and how to identify and control them. You should also be familiar with horticulture, plant relationships, and plant pests as they relate to agriculture. The median salary for entomologists in 2004 was about $48,000.

Entomology Field Assistants. Working alongside entomologists are entomology field assistants, who aid in trapping, fumigating, and spraying insects. They also supervise work crews and keep records. Often their work includes writing reports about their fieldwork.

With some work experience, assistants can survey infestations, track insect populations, evaluate control programs, and measure results. As with most environmental workers, field assistants are called upon to work with other specialists and technicians in government agencies and agriculture-related businesses.

You need at least two years of agriculture-related work to obtain an entry-level position as an entomology field assistant. Some of this experience should include work on insect control projects. You would have to know about pest control methods and equipment, which may include spray guns and turbine blowers. Your career probably would be with local and state government agencies, and you could work your way up with additional experience.

Plant Physiologists

Plant physiologists divide their work between the field and the laboratory. They conduct research on pesticides and then apply it to agricultural crops and plants. Plant physiologists also investigate the toxicity of pesticides and chemicals that are applied to agriculture.

If you worked for the government, you might advise manufacturers about the safety of new pesticides before they are labeled. Or you might testify at public hearings or in court as an expert witness. As with most scientists working with the natural environment, you might work with other scientists, technicians, agricultural extension service workers, and various other professionals.

To be a plant physiologist, you need an undergraduate degree. You should major in plant physiology but study all the biological sciences. Without work experience, you would then be qualified for an entry-level position. The more work experience and education you have, the better chance you will have for increased responsibilities and salary. As an outdoor lover, your best career opportunities are with state or provincial and local governments, although many plant physiologists teach and conduct research at the university level. Plant physiologists in 2004 earned a median salary of $60,000.

Agricultural Scientists

The work of agricultural scientists and technicians is with food production and processing; they may test crops for quality and yield, or they may test plants and animals for resistance to insects and disease. In so doing, they have to monitor experiments and evaluate results. Most of their work is done outdoors and is often dangerous, since they may be working with toxic substances or diseased organisms.

Agricultural science biologists need a bachelor's degree in biological sciences. You would have to take at least ten semester hours in plant biology and ten in vertebrate biology. In addition, you would have to be knowledgeable in botany, zoology, and mammalogy; botanical and zoological classification; pest control methods; and agriculture-related pest problems. Expect to take additional courses in math, economics, and English. You may also want to work in nurseries or seed fields, where you'd study insects and plants and serve as consultant to agricultural businesses. Or you could work at border control stations, inspecting and advising on regulations relating to agricultural imports and exports. This can occur at the borders between counties, states, provinces, and countries. Agricultural scientists are needed throughout the world, but you can contact the U.S. Department of Agriculture (www.usda.gov) or Agriculture and Agri-Food Canada (www.agr.gc.ca) about federal jobs. State, provincial, and local governments are also good sources for jobs, as well as agricultural experiment stations and agribusiness.

Median annual earnings for U.S. agricultural and food scientists ran about $51,000 in 2004. Job prospects appear solid in the midterm, with biotechnology pushing the envelope, demand for improved production high, and insects' resistance to existing pesticides calling for new solutions.

Veterinarians

Veterinarians are employed by the U.S. Department of Agriculture, the U.S. Food and Drug Administration, and Agriculture and Agri-Food Canada. In some cases, when they are working in the agricultural sciences, veterinarians try to improve breeding and livestock management or study diseases and insects that affect farm animals, including poultry. Agricultural experiment stations at public universities also employ veterinarians.

The demand for veterinarians who specialize in the public health sector, which includes agriculture, seems to be growing because the animal population is growing, in part because breeding methods have improved. Salaries vary according to the location of a practice and work experience, but the median salary for veterinarians was about $67,000 in 2004, and starting salaries, whether for large-animal or small-animal specialists, averaged about $51,000 in the same year.

If you choose to work with farm animals, your work would involve preventive care, vaccinations, and consultation with the farmer on feeding and production issues. In some cases, you would have to take care of wounds and fractures and perform surgery. Birthing of animals and artificial insemination may also be part of your practice.

Your prospects for a job working with farm animals should be better than in a small-animal practice because most graduates prefer not to work in rural areas. You may also consider employment as a livestock inspector who checks for transmissible diseases and, when found, quarantines animals. You may also inspect meat, poultry, or egg products at slaughterhouses or test live animals and carcasses for disease.

A doctor of veterinary medicine (DVM) degree from an accredited college and a license are required to practice. Preveterinary course work includes forty-five to ninety undergraduate semester hours, with emphasis on the sciences—a battery of courses just as rigorous as that for future MDs. Veterinary colleges offer courses in organic chemistry, physics, biochemistry, and general biology. In order to be accepted to your veterinary college of choice, you may also have to submit your test scores from the Graduate Record Examination (GRE), the Veterinary College Admission Test (VCAT), or the Medical College Admission Test (MCAT). Formal or volunteer experience with farm animals will give you a leg up on the competition, which is very intense. There are only twenty-eight accredited veterinary colleges in the United States and four in Canada.

If you live in Canada and you want to obtain a DVM degree, you must have a minimum of six years of university education with two years of preveterinary study in your undergraduate years. For more information about the veterinary profession in

Canada, contact the Canadian Veterinarian Medical Association (www.canadianveterinarians.net).

Chemists

If your specialty is chemistry, you could also become involved in agriculture. Because of the many pollutants in the environment, organic, inorganic, analytical, and physical chemists are needed to work in connection with government agencies and other agricultural scientists. You would probably divide your work between the field and the laboratory, primarily helping to enforce the laws that ensure safety in the manufacture of chemicals used in agriculture. In the laboratory, you would examine pesticides, analyzing them to see if they are toxic. Then you would determine under which conditions and dosages they pollute or contaminate. You would have to collect samples in the field and then follow certain scientific procedures to evaluate solutions. In your analysis and evaluation, you would deal with pesticides, fertilizers, residues, and feed. Since your work directly involves public health, you may be called on to present your findings at public hearings and evaluate the environmental impact of pesticides and chemicals.

Chemists need a degree in chemistry or biochemistry. Work experience of one or two years may also be required for some jobs if you don't have a master's or doctoral degree. You could find employment with the government or in industry, as either an agricultural chemist or environmental chemist. Salaries vary according to academic degree, work experience, and private- or public-sector employment. The median salary for chemists in 2004 was $56,000.

Chemical Technicians

Chemical technicians work alongside chemists in the manufacturing process or on the farm. They should have a background in applied chemistry, mathematics, and basic laboratory equipment. These skills can be acquired at an accredited college or in a two-year program. Junior or community colleges, some trade or technical schools, and four-year colleges offer the necessary courses. You may get further training on the job, but employers are increasingly looking for technicians with a two-year degree rather than unskilled workers who have to be completely trained on the job. Other chemical technicians have bachelor's degrees in chemistry or have taken several science and math courses at four-year colleges. The median hourly wage for chemical technicians in the United States in 2004 was $18.35.

Biotechnologists

Biotechnologists are also needed in agriculture and pesticide work. Biotechnology applies the disciplines of biochemistry, chemistry, microbiology, and chemical engineering to a wide variety of products and processes. Biotechnologists investigate ways to improve crops through alteration of genes so that plants manufacture their own natural pesticides. They also work on producing plants with more nutrition, improved hardiness against the elements, and more attractive appearances.

Call for an Agricultural Reformation

We can now see, from viewing these career possibilities, that planting food and bringing it to harvest, guaranteeing the health of plants and animals, and using the soil wisely is a very complex operation. Growing plants and animals depends on clean air and water, suitable soil, and nutritional feed and fertilizers. Farming in North America no longer resembles a Norman Rockwell illustration of a nuclear family tilling the ancestral plot generation after generation. Pollution, advanced technology, agribusiness, and harmful pesticides and chemicals have made dealing with the food chain very complicated. Many farmers have opted for organic methods in order to completely avoid the hazards of applying pesticides to crops.

In an area as vital as agriculture, it is essential that all scientists and technicians work together with the farmer, rancher, consumer, and government agencies to provide safe food today and improved crops for tomorrow. Our country and the world's population are in critical need of good food, equitably distributed. Highly educated and trained professionals are needed. They should be knowledgeable in their fields and have some familiarity with computers, satellites, and telemetry instruments. Interdisciplinary cooperation and application of mathematics, communication skills, social sciences, critical thinking, and analytical skills are necessary to make it all happen. Laboratory workers will have to share information with fieldworkers, chemists with biologists, biotechnologists with agronomists, soil scientists with pest control specialists. Plant and animal physiologists will share information with ecologists and crop specialists; federal, state, provincial, and local agencies will have to enforce laws concerning labeling and use of agricultural products. Consumers will have to be aware of the consequences of all of these processes and demand the safety of all foods that are consumed by animals and humans. Smart, dedicated people have made great strides in lifting the world's indigent out of poverty and ameliorating famines, but more must be done to ensure reasoned, sustainable food production for all and to manage it with care for the larger environment.

Agricultural Organizations

A wealth of professional and academic organizations offer information about agricultural careers, some of which are listed in the Appendix. Below are just a few that are doing important work in the field, both in terms of science and society, and they are good references for someone preparing to enter the field. Their websites variously offer job listings, professional news, updates about organization events, and e-newsletters.

American Society of Agronomy

The American Society of Agronomy (www.agronomy.org) is an international professional organization blending advancements in crop science with care for and preservation of the surrounding environment. Based in Madison, Wisconsin, the society offers professional certification, undergraduate- and graduate-level scholarships, and fellowships, and weighs in on policy through its Washington, D.C., office. The headquarters shares an office and staff with the Crop Science Society of America (www.crops.org) and the Soil Science Society of America (www.soils.org), two independent organizations with related goals.

Farm Animal Reform Movement

For every government agency or industry involved with agriculture, there are as many independent agencies seeking protection of animals on factory farms and in agribusiness. One such organization is the Farm Animal Reform Movement (FARM; www.farmusa.org), which is based in the United States but has members all over the world. The organization sponsors the annual Great American Meatout, when Americans are urged not to eat meat for one day. FARM encourages consumers to make the transition to vegetarian diets, raises awareness about abuse of farmed animals, including those used in the fur industry, and supports legislation for the humane treatment of animals.

Humane Farming Association

Another organization is the Humane Farming Association (www.hfa.org), well known for its campaign against the effects of factory farming on the quality of meat produced in the United States. It has documented many abuses in corporate farming through video recordings, still photography, and on-site observations from veterinarians and other experts and has created exposés to publicize the conditions. It also maintains a refuge for animals removed from abusive farm operations, the Suwanna Ranch in California.

With so many advancements and challenges in the field, the future in many aspects of agriculture should be bright, complex, exciting, and personally rewarding. No matter which path you take, education, training, and a willingness to get your hands dirty will help you carve out a career.

CHAPTER FIVE

Land Use Planning Careers

For the most part, North Americans haven't appreciated the true value of the land the way people have in more crowded places such as Japan and Europe, where the most is made of every meter, and public transit is second nature. But as the population closer to home continues to surge upward, energy challenges make oil-based transportation impractical, ongoing fragmentation of habitat imperils wildlife, and people search out places with a sense of community and vibrancy, smart land use choices will take on renewed importance.

Decisions about land use take place every day, from the lowest levels of municipal government to various federal departments, and from the urban core to the corn fields. These decisions tend to get made behind the scenes, and if we're aware of them at all, it's after the fact. Yet their effects can be profound. Once approval is granted for an agricultural plot to be rezoned as industrial, or for the rerouting of a highway, the impacts can't easily be reversed.

The Big Picture

Those who make their livings shaping the land know well the effects of certain types of uses. The land simply is not infinite; natural resources can be depleted if they are not used carefully and conserved. The soil can be contaminated, making it useless for growing or grazing. The plants and animals that depend on the earth for sustenance and, indeed, existence are in danger of extinction if their natural habitats are destroyed, and the extinction of any species upsets the ecological balance. Biologists, geologists, chemists, and other environmental professionals must work together to ensure a healthy and wholesome life for all living things. And all natural organisms are interdependent and must function as a team to survive. There is no hidden or secret nearby planet that can support life systems as we know them, so we have to take some serious steps to use appropriately the land that we still have, to consider all requests for its use, and to work toward an equitable solution for its proper use.

U.S. Government Agencies and Laws

Local and federal laws help maintain public lands, and some government agencies are charged with protecting and preserving land-based natural resources. The Department of Interior's U.S. Geological Survey (www.usgs.gov), National Park Service (www.nps.gov), Bureau of Land Management (www.blm.gov), and Bureau of Reclamation (www.usbr.gov) all have responsibilities for—and therefore employment possibilities in—land use and planning. The Forest Service (www.fs.fed.us), part of the Department of Agriculture, as well as municipal and state governments, employs land planners, landscape architects, surveyors, landscape designers, and plant scientists.

The National Park Service and U.S. Forest Service

The National Park Service and the U.S. Forest Service have been around since the beginning of the twentieth century, but increased awareness of the environment occurred in the 1970s, when laws were passed and agencies established to set and enforce standards. The National Environmental Policy Act requires environmental impact statements for any project that will affect human life. The

Endangered Species Act and the Federal Surface Mining and Reclamation Act were also established during that time. Land use is a contentious issue in national parks, where the number of visitors rises continually and the NPS struggles to furnish the amenities visitors expect without contradicting their mandate to preserve the land for future generations.

The Federal Highway Administration

The Federal Highway Administration (www.fhwa.dot.gov) ensures the safety and efficiency of U.S. highways, overseeing policy, planning, research, design, construction, and maintenance of the highway transportation system. It also administers the Federal Lands Highway Program, which oversees the survey, design, and construction of federal highways and access roads in forests, on Indian reservations, and for defense. The Federal Lands Highway Program supplies engineering services to plan, design, construct, and rehabilitate highways and bridges that access federally owned lands.

The Highway Administration has cooperative agreements with the National Park Service and the Bureau of Indian Affairs (www.doi.gov/bureau-indian-affairs.html) to coordinate programs and funding for more than ninety thousand miles of federally owned roads. It employs about six hundred workers in Washington, D.C.; Sterling, Virginia; Lakewood, Colorado; and Vancouver, Washington. Other partnerships include the Bureau of Land Management, Federal Aviation Administration (www.faa.gov), National Park Service, U.S. Army Corps of Engineers (www.usace.army.mil), U.S. Forest Service, U.S. Department of Transportation (www.dot.gov), and state and local governments.

The Environmental Protection Agency

The Environmental Protection Agency (EPA; www.epa.gov) was established in 1970 by merging several other departments and agencies. The idea was to have a unified national program to solve environmental problems rather than rely on a wide variety of local ordinances throughout the country. The EPA safeguards the air and water against pesticides, noise, wastewater, solid waste, toxic substances, and radiation in the United States. It is responsible for policy, standards, support, and evaluation of environmental factors through its regional offices. The EPA is also responsible for enforcement of environmental regulations.

The National Environmental Policy Act

In 1970, the National Environmental Policy Act (NEPA) became law. It was meant to establish a balance between human needs and the natural environment. Because of NEPA, the Council on Environmental Quality (www.whitehouse.gov/ceq) was conceived to help the president determine sound environmental policy on a national basis. This council makes it necessary for all federal agencies to prepare environmental impact statements before they begin any major project, including construction of nuclear power plants, highways, and bridges.

A report on all potential consequences is then given to federal, state, and local agencies for review and approval. After every responsible jurisdiction has commented on, objected to, revised, and resolved the problems, the EPA receives a copy, which then becomes available to the public.

These statements are extremely detailed and include probable and indirect effects on the ecology of a given area, short-term and long-term evaluations, and any possibilities of irretrievable damage to all aspects of the environment. And although the EPA cannot legally prevent another federal agency from going ahead with a project, it has the responsibility to advise the other agencies and the public of the environmental consequences.

These environmental impact statements can be crucial to land planners and architects. Further legislation that also affects land use planners are the Coastal Zone Management Act, the Resource

Conservation and Recovery Act, the Clean Air Act, and the Safe Drinking Water Act.

Canadian Government Agencies and Laws

Although most planning jobs are at the municipal or provincial levels, Canada's environmental regulations do present opportunities for planners to work at the federal level. The country's emphasis on sustainability requires careful analysis from staff at Environment Canada and the Canadian Environmental Assessment Agency, for example.

Environment Canada

Environment Canada (www.ec.gc.ca), once known as the Department of the Environment, has a responsibility to oversee the country's environmental programs and regulations, spearhead cleanups following environmental disasters, and conduct research on environmental threats, such as global warming. It has a broad reach, and one of its major focuses is sustainability. The agency aims to minimize the impact of development and pollution where possible.

Canadian Environmental Assessment Agency (CEAA)

Independent of Environment Canada, the CEAA (www.ceaa-acee .gc.ca) ensures compliance with the Canadian Environmental Protection Act (CEPA), which, similar to the National Environmental Policy Act of the United States, requires federal departments and agencies to conduct environmental impact statements for any project undertaken by the federal government or for projects for which the federal government issues permits or provides funding. Updated in 1999, the CEPA has as its primary goal the prevention of pollution and the careful management of existing toxic wastes, particularly those that do not easily biodegrade and tend to accumulate in soil, water, and wildlife. The ultimate goal, however, is the protection of Canadians' health and the perpetuation of a sustainable society.

Land Planners

Because the land in all its various forms is used for many purposes, land planners are needed for city and regional planning, residential subdivisions, rural areas, parks, and forests. Highways and housing developments, shopping malls and golf courses, airports and recreation areas all require the work of land planners.

Site planning involves collaborations with architects, engineers, surveyors, and environmental specialists to develop commercial, residential, recreational, and industrial projects. Natural land planning involves environmental engineers, forest managers, and wildlife biologists. Wildlife, plants, and nature trails may be designed into a development through the skilled use of a planning team. Civil engineers, surveyors, and landscape architects work with environmental specialists for storm water management, road design, and erosion control.

Planners have to know about local zoning regulations, pollution control laws, and building codes. Projects have to be approved by utility companies, zoning agencies, and city, state, and federal agencies to obtain permits for planned development. Planners are responsible for taking in all points of view, such as the real estate developer's, the historic preservation professional's, the engineer's, and the local citizenry's, and coming up with an environmentally balanced plan. Besides land issues, the planner also considers air and water safety. In addition to all these factors, economic and social problems are part of the mix.

After initial discussions with the concerned parties, land planners study analyses of the soil, water, and air as well as any other natural resources that will be affected by the project. These may include plants, wildlife, insects, trees, rivers, and lakes. The land planner must be mindful of the project's goals at this stage. For example, the goals of rehabilitating an urban neighborhood would be different from those of an interstate highway construction. The land surrounding that under consideration also must be investigated.

Three-dimensional modeling and mapping software has come far in helping planners develop theoretical digital landscapes to analyze the maze of factors and interests in a project and create workable plans. Drawing from geographic information systems (GIS) databases, planners can inject data into a digital modeling software program, such as Autodesk, to determine how particular structures might be used, where they should be positioned, and even what the environmental impacts might be. The U.S. military has used this type of technology before entering battle zones to formulate strategy and show soldiers what to expect. The same GIS data allows planners to extrapolate to future land uses so that civic projects can account for growth and change. They can also analyze potential impacts on neighboring properties.

Land planners work with diverse populations using a wide variety of skills, including analysis, communication, diplomacy, and economics. If you decide to become a land planner, you may prepare yourself during college, planning an educational track that includes a master's degree. Your undergraduate major could be in planning, environmental studies, or urban studies, with a curriculum that includes civil engineering, public administration, landscape architecture, natural science, and public health. Round out your college studies with some social sciences, such as economics, political science, law, geography, and a strong base in both oral and written communications. Try to develop strong decision-making and problem-solving skills as well as critical-thinking abilities.

If you have the opportunity during your summer breaks, get a job at the planning department in your hometown, attend public hearings on land use projects, volunteer at the local zoning board, or work on a neighborhood rehabilitation project.

If you already have your undergraduate degree and are working in a related field, you still will need a master's degree, and it would also be a good idea to get some work experience in zoning, geography, resource economics, or urban planning.

As you begin your job search, you may want to take a geographic approach; that is, find out where the jobs are and be willing to relocate in order to start your career. This approach might increase your chances of finding what you want. However, because of the need for land planners, you may very well be able to stay where you are and find a job with your local government, historic preservation group, or consulting group.

If you work in a small town, you may be required to do everything—that is, take the project from beginning to end. In a large city, you may be more specialized and departmentalized and work under the instruction and supervision of a more experienced planner.

The recognized professional organization for land planners is the American Planning Association (www.planning.org). Members are entitled to a job-listing service and publications on salary trends. Salaries, of course, will vary from state to state and agency to agency, but the median salary for U.S. planners, according to the American Planning Association, is $63,700.

Land planning offers a rather bright future for people who are creative, analytical, proficient in communications skills, well versed in public policy and legislation, and dedicated to the goal of achieving environmental harmony and balance between humans, animals, and plants and the aesthetic and economic needs of the community.

Landscape Architects

Working closely with the land planner is the landscape architect. According to the American Society of Landscape Architects (www.asla.org), there are about twenty-five thousand landscape architects now working in the United States, with most of those employed by architectural, landscape architectural, engineering, and landscaping services. State and local governments are the next-largest employers.

Landscape architects play a vital role in the preservation of the environment by designing, planning, and managing the land. They are concerned not only with the beauty of the design but also with environmental impact and the best use of the land.

Much like land planners, landscape architects work in urban, suburban, and rural settings, in parks, housing developments, and national forests, and on regional projects. They must be able to solve problems, work with other professionals and community groups, speak and write English well, be proficient in graphic design, and have a deep commitment to the environment.

Landscape architects have to know about soil erosion, plant and animal relationships, and noise-absorbing vegetation. They usually spend a great deal of time on the site they're designing the landscaping for, whether it's a recreational facility, airport, highway, subdivision, industrial park, or shopping mall. They may work for the municipal planning agency, a national park or forest, a consulting firm, or a developer. They work with planners, engineers, architects, and natural scientists, such as plant and animal physiologists.

In the process of their on-site analyses, they study the geography, topography, climate, and position of existing structures, such as buildings or bridges. They often use the increasingly potent 3-D modeling software that allows landscape architects to test designs before breaking ground. All details, such as roadways, parking facilities, walls, and fences, are included in these models.

Landscape architects also use working models made of sand or clay as a transitional design step between paper and reality.

Communication skills play a role because they have to prepare written reports, usually with detailed graphics, and make oral presentations on the feasibility of a particular project. Creativity and highly developed technical skills are needed at this stage of the process.

If you were the one in the family who liked to do the yard work, mow the lawn, plant the flower and vegetable gardens, trim the bushes, and prune the trees, you may be perfect for this line of work. But in addition to this basic aptitude, you need a minimum of a college degree, usually a bachelor's degree in landscape architecture.

As an undergraduate, you would take natural and social sciences, behavioral sciences, art, mathematics, surveying, landscape design and construction, landscape ecology, site design, and urban and rural planning. You might also study plant and soil science, geology, and general management. English, math, physical science courses, and work in a design studio would also enhance your qualifications. The bachelor's degree usually takes four to five years. Graduates can pursue a master's in landscape architecture, which is the minimum necessary if you want to be a university lecturer or engage in specialized research. For the master's degree, there are two choices: a professional three-year program for those with a bachelor's degree in another field, or a two-year professional degree for those who already have a bachelor's in landscape architecture.

The accrediting agencies for programs in landscape architecture are the Landscape Architectural Accreditation Board of the American Society of Landscape Architects (www.asla.org/nonmembers/education/laab.htm) and the Canadian Society of Landscape Architects Accreditation Council (www.csla.ca). There are forty-five accredited undergraduate and thirty-nine accredited graduate programs between the two countries, with the great majority of these in the United States.

You'll also need to determine what your state requires in addition to your degree for granting a license to practice. Only Colorado, Vermont, and the District of Columbia don't have licensing requirements. State requirements vary, so it may be difficult to transfer your registration from state to state. In Canada, only British Columbia and Ontario require licensing, which is reciprocal between those provinces. Licensing usually consists of passing an examination and may also include some supervised practice. In order to be licensed, you must know about laws and environmental regulations, as well as about plants and soils indigenous to the particular state. Federal agencies do not require licensing.

Finding a Job

Many landscape architects are self-employed or work for small firms. Therefore, benefits may not be generous. Others work in architectural and engineering firms or with the government. The U.S. government's primary employers of landscape architects are the departments of Agriculture, Defense, and Interior; the Forest Service; and the National Park Service. Work as a landscape architect is done in the office or at the worksite, and the hours are fairly regular, unless a deadline necessitates some overtime.

After you have had several years of experience, you may become a project manager, associate, or partner. Salaries vary according to your experience and your employer, whether private or governmental. The median salary for landscape architects in 2004 was $53,000. For those working for the U.S. government in 2005, the figure was $74,500.

Mapping-Related Careers

As you can see, land planning, design, and management are possible only when various dedicated professionals share information; analyze data; and make wise, safe, and healthy decisions based on ecological systems. For example, the land planner works with the realty specialist, investigates all aspects of selling or leasing land, arranges for permits, and submits studies on the proper use of the land. Realty specialists may work with geologists (see Chapter 6) who have mapped the area that is being considered for use. The geologist uses maps that show minerals and bedrock in the area being considered for use and analyzes data collected from the actual site. They may all work with a cartographer, who designs maps of a specific area from aerial photos and other larger maps. All of these professionals depend on the work of the surveyor, who must be aware of the boundaries within which the project is to be constructed. With the help of surveyors, property disputes are avoided or ironed out based on titles and legal claims to the land.

Geographers

Geographers, who are versed in both the natural and social sciences, are being called on more and more for their expertise in land use problems. They study not only the location of natural phenomena, but also the reason for that location. They analyze both physical and cultural aspects with emphasis on interpreting the ever-changing environment.

Geographers are employed by government and private agencies to research urban renewal, resource management, and highway systems. Sophisticated techniques used by contemporary geographers include remote sensing and statistical analyses to promote wise land use.

Those geographers who specialize in landforms and soil erosion may be called on to help in city planning or regional planning where geographic considerations are at stake. Geographers are uniquely qualified to study human relationships in regard to their physical environment. Becoming a geographer might interest you if you

- like to study maps
- are curious about other places and foreign countries
- like to work outside

* are a problem solver
* are technologically grounded
* want to make a connection between human life and the natural environment

If you study geography, you might work as a cartographer, land officer, consulting biologist, environmental engineer, planner, or soil conservationist. Private businesses employ geographers to help them locate new industrial sites or plan transportation systems. City and county planners employ geographers in growing numbers because they often determine environmental considerations and risks.

Professional geographers need a bachelor's degree in geography, with emphasis on statistical methods, computers, cartography, communication skills, foreign language, environmental studies, field techniques, meteorology, climatology, and map design and interpretation. Additional course work might include oceanography, human geography, geomorphology, and environmental geography.

If you desire a better-paying job, consider obtaining a master's degree, which will include an internship plus thirty to thirty-six semester or forty-five to fifty-four quarter hours. The median salary for all U.S. geographers in 2004 was $59,000. The entry-level salary range in the U.S. government was about $30,500 for those with a bachelor's degree, $37,000 with a master's, and $45,000 with a doctorate.

The federal government employs geographers at the National Geospatial-Intelligence Agency (www.nga.mil), the Bureau of the Census (www.census.gov), and the U.S. Geological Survey (USGS; www.usgs.gov). The USGS website offers job listings, maps, a huge publications database, and numerous educational resources. Canadians can look to the Geological Survey of Canada (www.gsc.nrcan.gc.ca) for agency publications, downloadable maps, and educational resources. The professional organization for geographers is the Association of American Geographers (www.aag.org). Membership includes regional events, a newsletter, job resources, and access to a grants program.

Geographic Information Systems (GIS) Specialist

Many land use professionals use computer systems that store, display, analyze, and map information. Geographers, land planners, and government officials use the GIS to evaluate transportation systems, traffic, environmental problems, soil, and flood zones so that they can make appropriate decisions. The median U.S. salary for a nonmanager GIS specialist in 2006 was about $48,000. You might also like to work with the Department of Agriculture (www.usda.gov), Department of Defense (www.defenselink.mil), the State Department (www.state.gov), or the Central Intelligence Agency (www.cia.gov) to interpret photos as a remote-sensing analyst.

Cartographers

Cartographers design, compile, and reproduce maps. Charting maps of land areas is done digitally. The federal government needs people to fill all these job categories through the Bureau of Land Management or the U.S. Geological Survey, both units of the Department of the Interior. At the GS-5 level, you would need a bachelor's degree or a combination of education (thirty semester hours in cartography) and related work experience. If you want to qualify with your bachelor's degree alone, you need at least thirty semester hours of cartography, related physical science, computer science, or physical geography. In addition, you would need at least six semester hours of scientific math. If you choose to work for the government, you might also find career opportunities at the Bureau of the Census, the National Geospatial-Intelligence Agency, the Federal Highway Administration, the U.S. Army Corps of Engineers, the U.S. Forest Service, or the Tennessee

Valley Authority (www.tva.gov). Canadian agencies that hire cartographers include the Geological Survey of Canada, the National Defence and the Canadian Forces (www.forces.gc.ca), Natural Resources Canada (www.nrcan-rncan.gc.ca), and the Canada Centre for Remote Sensing (www.ccrs.nrcan.gc.ca).

To prepare for a career in cartography, take college courses in the principles of cartography, remote sensing, computer mapping, map design, and geographic information systems (GIS) and learn to draw, read, and interpret maps. Drawing by hand is a good skill to have, but today's cartographers perform their work with graphics software. In addition to a bachelor's degree, a good internship and membership in a professional association can help you get started. Cartographers earned a median salary of $46,000 in 2004.

The Land Planner as Caretaker

These are some of the careers available to you if you want to work on planning, designing, preserving, and understanding the land and its relationship to human needs and nature's ecological demands. The land is inspiring and peaceful, but we have to work to keep it that way. Natural beauty *can* be cultivated and enhanced. It can be saved from further destruction and can provide recreational, residential, and commercial space for millions.

Municipal planners know that our natural resources can be safe havens for the many residents who are so used to concrete, brick, glass, and steel as everyday environments. Parks, gardens, and green spaces can be incorporated into new and existing city plans for rejuvenation and rehabilitation of the urban environment. Even when new buildings must be built, the total natural environment must not be destroyed to accommodate them. Planners and architects know how to coordinate human needs with the needs of other species that also depend on the land for survival.

Technicians are responsible for preserving and maintaining the land; geologists, geographers, surveyors, and cartographers are called on for resource development, often for larger regional projects sponsored by the federal government. Understanding the land and its various functions, plotting it for possible use, understanding interrelationships, and interpreting pertinent data are some of their responsibilities. All work closely with land planners and landscape architects.

So if the land is your passion, you will have various opportunities to plan and preserve it with these careers. If you are creative and appreciate the many facets of human life and the diversity of other species, land planning or landscape architecture may be for you.

Now you'll have to decide which career path interests you most, how much time you want to devote to education and training, and maybe even how much physical work you may want to do. Some of these jobs involve working closely with others from different areas of expertise; some require supervisory skills. Others rely more on physical strength.

Many of these career opportunities are available through municipal, state, provincial, and federal governmental agencies. However, private associations and organizations, although they may not have large staffs, are good sources of information about specific areas of land preservation. See the Appendix to find associations dealing with the career path you're interested in. You may wish to contact them to help you get started in your career search. They may also have volunteer programs on a limited basis.

Whichever career you choose, you will know that you are playing a vital role in the preservation of the earth's beauties in all their forms. And you will help create a better, more attractive world for generations to come.

Geoscience Careers

eoscientist is an umbrella term for people who study the physical, material elements of earth rather than the living organisms that populate it. Perhaps the best known among them are geologists, who peel back the earth's topmost organic layer to expose the secrets lying in the rocks underneath. But geoscientists study more than just rock formations. Some deal with the atmosphere, the oceans, or the earth's magnetic field. Geophysicists are geoscientists. So are hydrologists and oceanographers. (Oceanographers, the interdisciplinary scientists who might also study marine life, are covered in Chapter 2, "Bioscience Careers.") They address the big picture through the ages, as when studying the fossil record for an entire geologic era, and the here and now, like petroleum geologists who search for oil or natural gas deposits.

Because of the power of their analyses and the broad applications for their findings, geoscientists work in a remarkable variety of settings, many of them outdoors. They're useful in mining and drilling for their expertise in identifying productive sites and determining the best way to extract. Engineering geologists work in both industry and government on major construction projects, such as dams and tunnels, to ensure the structure's viability, integrity, and safety. Other geoscientists study, preserve, and clean the environment. They observe strict environmental regulations by monitoring waste disposal sites and working to reclaim polluted land and water. They also might try to predict the planet's systems, find natural resources, conserve soils, and determine geological controls on natural resources. They study the earth's past in order to predict its future.

Geoscientists are globetrotters and frequently work in the field. The unusual sites and formations that geoscientists focus on might be hours or days away, on land or in the sea. The complex equipment required for fieldwork can mean carrying loads to remote sites on foot. More and more geoscientists are traveling outside of North America to work—it is, after all, a global science—so knowing a foreign language could be useful in your career. As we've already discussed, many geoscientists work in private industry, but in the United States a quarter of them work for the government, many of them with the U.S. Geological Survey.

The sciences often require advanced degrees, and geoscience is no exception. A professional geoscientist needs at least a master's degree to enter the field, and many have doctorates, a prerequisite for research and teaching positions. If you're an analytical problem solver with a talent for math and physics as well as science, and if earth science and the outdoors hold strong appeal for you, geoscience could be the path for you. About one hundred U.S. universities offer undergraduate degree programs in the geosciences, with another forty-plus in Canada, indicating the specialized nature of the subject. The relatively high educational bar does translate into less competition for the available jobs.

Geologists

Geologists study the earth's composition, evolution, past, and future. They do this by investigating rocks and fossils, continental shifts, and natural resources. Depending on your inclinations, you could become an economic, engineering, glacial, marine, or environmental geologist. Economic geologists study mineral deposits and explore ways to safely dispose of waste as a result of mining. Glacial geologists study glaciers and ice sheets, and marine geologists study the ocean floor and basins and coastal environments.

Environmental geologists study the geosphere, hydrosphere, atmosphere, and biosphere in order to find out how pollution, waste management, and natural disasters affect human life. The federal agencies that are most likely to employ geologists are the U.S. Department of the Interior (www.doi.gov), which includes the U.S. Geological Survey (www.usgs.gov) and the Bureau of Reclamation (www.usbr.gov); the departments of Defense (www.defenselink.mil), Agriculture (www.usda.gov), Energy (www.doe.gov), and Commerce (www.commerce.gov); and the Environmental Protection Agency (www.epa.gov).

In Canada, departments employing geologists include Environment Canada (www.ec.gc.ca), Natural Resources Canada (www.nrcan-rncan.gc.ca), and its subunit, the Geological Survey of Canada (www.gsc.nrcan.gc.ca). With some experience, you may even be able to work as a private consultant.

You would have to be physically strong and like to work under all kinds of climatic conditions to be a geologist. In the field, you would need keen observation skills in all aspects of your work. You would be using tools, collecting samples, and measuring. You may also be called on to design computer models to test theories. Geologists in the field usually work together in groups or in teams and have to be able to get along with other people.

If you're still in high school and want to pursue geology, you should have a firm footing in math and science and study English and foreign languages. Recommended college courses include chemistry, physics, biology, engineering, and math in addition to geology. Further study may include hydrology, geophysics, petrology, marine geology, or even paleontology. Many colleges and universities in the United States and Canada offer degrees in geology (see www.ccpg.ca/links/university_departments.html), but you should check the requirements and curricula before you select a college or university for undergraduate work.

The highest salaries for geologists are often found in the private sector; government generally has a somewhat lower pay scale.

Salaries vary, of course, but the median salary for an entry-level geologist with a master's degree was about $41,000 in 2004.

You may want to work with a state, provincial, or county agency as a volunteer or part-time worker to see whether geology is for you. Since geologists work with other scientists and professionals, you could work in a local park or forest with surveyors or cartographers, urban land planners, or engineers during your summer breaks or vacations.

You might also work for a local waste management firm, seismologist, oceanographer, or mineralogist. This part-time or volunteer work can also give you a better idea about job opportunities in the various areas of specialization in the agency or industry you choose. Employers prefer applicants with field experience, so a summer internship may also be beneficial. Your education and training will be your best assets in finding a job. Today's geologists, like other geoscientists, need to have experience with computer modeling, data analysis and integration, digital mapping, remote sensing, and geographic information systems such as the Geographic Information Systems (GIS) and the Global Positioning System (GPS).

Professional organizations are also helpful for finding your niche in the work world. Primary among them are the American Geological Institute (www.agiweb.org), the American Association of Petroleum Geologists (www.aapg.org), the Geological Society of America (www.geosociety.org), and the Geological Association of Canada (www.gac.ca). These organizations can provide you with additional information in your search for rocks and fossils—and jobs.

As a nature-loving geologist, much of your effort in the future would be directed toward improvement of our natural resources, including cleaning up pollution in our water supply. Together with hydrologists and engineers, you would be called upon to contribute to the clean-up process.

Geophysicists

Geophysicists, who study the earth and apply the principles of physics to its atmosphere, oceans, and space environment, also work on environmental problems. They help find new sources of energy, understand the climate, study the ocean, and investigate the solar system. Geophysicists look for mineral deposits, study the earth's movements, and probe the evolution of oceans.

Geophysics also boasts a number of important subspecialties. Planetologists study the solar system to help us better understand the earth; seismologists study earthquakes and explosive shocks under the earth in order to understand their causes and better predict their occurrence; volcanologists study the nature of volcanoes and how they affect the earth's structure. These geophysicists all must have a solid grounding in mathematics and natural science. Like geologists, geophysicists also need computer skills. Physics, chemistry, and geology as well as differential calculus are necessary for any undergraduate course of study. You should have at least thirty semester hours in mathematics and the physical sciences. Twenty of those hours would include geophysics and physics or math.

Geophysicists should have a good general education because they must be flexible, resourceful, and often willing to travel abroad and work with other professionals. Essential skills include communications, the ability to work on a team, and facility in computer modeling, data analysis and integration, digital mapping, remote sensing, and geographic information systems. Your work may be in a laboratory or in the field.

Hydrologists

The environment demands committed work from a variety of professionals, and hydrologists play an integral part in the continuing efforts to maintain the quality of our water. Hydrologists study the location of water on the earth and how it behaves. They work in forestry, range management, public health, and energy development. They can be found in the mountains and deserts, on farms and in cities. Interrelationships with rocks, dynamics of bodies of water, surface and groundwater, moisture in the soil, sediment, and precipitation all fall in the boundaries of the hydrologists' work.

Their work is crucial to our knowledge and understanding of our water supply, how it is used, how much we have, and what forms it takes. Water might just be the most precious natural resource we will have in the decades to come. In the United States, the population continues to move west, to desert areas not naturally designed to support such large populations, even as the big dams and water reclamation projects of the twentieth century are being reversed. In many other parts of the world, such as India and Africa, poor sanitation and over-reliance on underground aquifers make clean water increasingly scarce. Only about 0.3 percent of Earth's water is usable freshwater.

Hydrologists measure bodies of water and check the amount of underground water, too. Since some of our water comes from snow and rain, hydrologists' work is connected to that of meteorologists. Hydrologists study water as it exists as a liquid, solid, or gas, and, therefore, they necessarily work with glaciers, ice, and snow, as well as oceans, lakes, and rivers. Since so much water runs through rocks, hydrologists often work with geologists.

Hydrologists collect water samples and analyze them for quantity and quality. They can recommend the most efficient use of the resources we have and predict future needs.

Included in water resource development are water conservation, water quality planning, and the protection of watersheds. Studying water pollution, predicting floods, solving water shortage problems, and forecasting drought are also within a hydrologist's purview.

Hydrologists' data also assist in solving water power, irrigation, crop production, and navigation problems. They may also assist in planning farm ponds, sewers, drainage systems, and dams. Erosion, sedimentary deposits, snowfall—all are part of the total picture that the hydrologist must investigate and analyze. So the hydrologist's work affects everyone's lives and contributes a great deal to the preservation of the environment.

If you become an oceanographic hydrologist, you could assist fishing, shipping, and mining enterprises. You could also be involved in international cooperative ventures since all countries are bound by common oceans and, in some cases, rivers and lakes. Much of your work would be outdoors and involve light to moderate physical work. Good eyesight, creativity, and the ability to share information and work well with others are valuable characteristics for hydrologists. Report writing would also be a part of your job, and, as with geologists and geophysicists, hydrologists need to make use of sophisticated computer processes, such as remote sensing technology, data assimilation, and numerical modeling to monitor the change in regional and global water cycles.

Hydrologists need to know, among other sciences, chemistry, soil science, engineering science, aquatic biology, atmospheric science, and hydrogeology, as well as math and water management. In some cases, graduates with a bachelor's degree in a hydrologic science are qualified for positions in environmental consulting and planning regarding water quality or wastewater treatment.

For either the private or public sector, you must have a bachelor's degree with thirty semester hours of course work, including any combination of hydrology, physical sciences, engineering science, soils, math, aquatic biology, and the management or conservation of water resources. Math courses should include differential and integral calculus and physics. The USGS recommends studying atmospheric science, meteorology, geology, oceanography, and atmospheric science. It may also accept an appropriate combination of education and experience. The American Institute of Hydrology (www.aihydro.org) offers certification programs in professional hydrology.

The Outlook for Geoscience Jobs

Overall the geosciences offer stable but not fast-growing job opportunities. Some positions will open up as older scientists retire. The advanced education required will restrict the competition among applicants somewhat, but limited government budgets combined with outsourcing of public jobs could erode those advantages. The most plentiful opportunities will be in the private sector, particularly in consulting. The oil industry, which accounts for about 40 percent of geoscience employment, is an up-and-down business with abrupt changes in staffing to match, but if oil supplies remain tight and gas prices relatively high, hiring for petroleum geologists will be strong.

Hydrology is an exception to the trend of slow growth in geoscience careers. The need to comply with environmental regulations and the inherent value of clean water are driving high growth for hydrology jobs, especially in flood control and water decontamination. The acute demand for hydrologists should continue until at least the mid-2010s. As in other areas of geoscience, consultants will see the largest gains in job growth. The median salary for hydrologists in 2004 was $62,000, while geologists and geophysicists earned a median salary of $69,000. Consultants and petroleum geologists enjoy higher salaries but also have less secure jobs.

The U.S. Geological Survey

The U.S. Geological Survey (USGS), the nation's largest science and civilian mapping agency, employs ten thousand people, many of them geoscientists, and addresses a striking array of issues and needs. The USGS monitors and analyzes all aspects of the country's geological phenomena, from volcanoes and seismic activity to disappearing glaciers and rising sea levels. One major responsibility is to track potential threats to public safety and keep government informed of the risks. It is also charged with helping protect the natural world and with furnishing related information to educate the public, as with the familiar topographic maps it updates and publishes for outdoor recreation.

The USGS fulfills its mission by maintaining national and regional databases, analyzing and assessing methods, and conducting research to help sustain adequate natural resources according to environmental standards. Assessment and analysis methods include remote sensing, meteorite research, and mine waste characterization. If this mission interests you, you may want to work for the USGS, a progressive and family-friendly agency for its employees.

In rough terms, a relevant bachelor's degree would qualify you to start at a GS-5 level. (See the "U.S. Government" section in Chapter 2 for descriptions of Government Service levels.) With some graduate-level schooling or a year of experience, you would qualify for the GS-7 level. The GS-9 level equates to a master's degree level, and GS-11 to a doctorate. Your salary would depend on your education, experience, and responsibilities. For a table of U.S. government pay levels, visit www.opm.gov/oca and click on "Salaries and Wages." Benefits include:

- flexible work schedules
- paid vacation, sick days, and national holidays
- group medical insurance
- a federal pension
- tuition assistance

Geological Survey of Canada

The Geological Survey of Canada (GSC), a division of Natural Resources Canada, has many of the same goals as the USGS

Survey. The GSC deals with aspects of economic development, such as mining and offshore drilling, public safety, and environmental concerns. With such diverse charges, the GSC's underlying mandate is the study of Canada's geology and the reporting of that information to other branches of Canada's government, its citizens, and the scientific community. Begun in 1842, the GSC is actually much older than its U.S. counterpart and shares a similar prestige in the world of science, although the agency is significantly smaller than the USGS.

The Geological Survey of Canada is a great place to work and should present good employment opportunities in the midterm. Its Targeted Geoscience Initiative commits $25 million through 2010 to strengthen base metal reserves in traditional Canadian mining communities, and part of its strategy includes offering research opportunities to both undergraduate and graduate students to boost knowledge and training in base metals. The program partners the GSC with industry and provincial geological survey programs. For more information, check out www.ess.nrcan.gc.ca/tgi/career_e.php. To search geoscientist jobs with the Canadian government, visit www.jobs-emplois.gc.ca. Many jobs are open to noncitizens.

Other Government Positions

State, provincial, and local governments need geoscientists to administer environmental laws at these levels. They also need people with geologic mapping skills; the ability to assess resources; and the ability to identify natural disasters such as tornadoes, volcanoes, and earthquakes. These governments may also provide opportunities for volunteer and part-time work, giving you a chance to explore the possibilities before you commit to the education and training that will be required for full-time employment as a geoscientist. Visit www.wmmf.org/links/links.shtml for links to worldwide geological surveys.

Business Positions

Geoscientists are also employed in private industry. You would probably be working in oil, gas, mining and minerals, or water resources. Some opportunities in private industry are for life scientists, chemists, meteorologists, soil scientists, and mapping scientists in the business of petroleum and natural gas exploration and extraction. Pay is higher in the private sector, but so is the competition. Also, there tends to be less job security in this sector as these industries are vulnerable to recessions and changes in oil and gas prices, among other factors, and they usually release workers when exploration and drilling slow down.

As government agencies contract for outside services more often, employment of private consultants will grow at a healthy clip. Consulting firms require master's degrees or bachelor's degrees with appropriate field experience. Geoscientists in general will also find employment in oil, gas, engineering, and construction companies.

Our workforce needs skilled professional people working to preserve the environment, and these same professionals are needed throughout the world, especially in developing countries that need the technological expertise that these scientists can provide. So it is appropriate that those people who work so closely with the resources of the earth should be able to work anywhere on the earth in order to solve resource problems.

CHAPTER SEVEN

Pollution Control Careers

N o one is isolated from environmental problems. They affect us all. Because pollution is a global problem, national governments have devised regulations and enforcements that seek to curb any further damage to the water, land, and air we depend on. Public-private partnerships help ensure a clean environment for future generations. States and provinces work with their respective federal governments, which also contract with industry to manage some elements of cleanup, and environmental organizations work with international agencies to resolve common problems. Watchdog groups look for inadequacies in governmental regulations and try to correct them.

Given that every community must in some way deal with pollution and waste, the field presents a great number of opportunities for a striking array of candidates, from high school graduates to Ph.D.s. Here we'll cover work in three main areas of pollution control: for water, for land, and for air.

Jobs in Water Pollution Control

Water pollution is one of the most serious problems that we face because water recycles itself. We have roughly the same amount of water today that we will a hundred or a thousand years from now, so we must be sure that what we put in the water won't be harmful to us or the plants and animals that depend on it down the road. This is a difficult task because we're continually finding out more about aquatic ecosystems and how certain contaminants can affect them, so even effectively regulating known pollutants doesn't guarantee us clean water. Furthermore, old toxins can settle into riverbeds, lakebeds, plants, and fish and other animals and cause problems decades after the source of the pollution has been eliminated.

Several laws do help us control damage to our waterways. In the United States there's the Water Quality Act, the Clean Water Act, and the Safe Drinking Water Act. Canada has the Canada Water Act and the Department of the Environment Act. All of this legislation provides standards of purity for interstate, coastal, and drinking water. These laws were passed to ensure that no industry could discharge pollutant material into water without permission and that waste material would be pretreated so as not to harm city treatment facilities. They also ensure the quality of the taste and odor of drinking water and mandate that drinking water be clean enough to avoid spreading disease.

Wastewater has to be treated for reuse in a treatment plant, usually through sewers. Solids are removed, and then the water is treated using bacteria in aerated tanks that break down organic material. Depending on the plant, the water might undergo a tertiary treatment with chemicals and filters that remove nitrogen and phosphorus; the plant adds chlorine to kill the rest of the bacteria and then discharges it into nearby bodies of water or, in some cases, provides it for irrigation.

Because of the expanding global population and resulting industrial waste, water pollution control will present steady job opportunities in the midterm. Again, a wide range of career opportunities awaits you, depending on the time you are willing to devote to education and training and whether you want to work for government, industry, or independent organizations. We divide career paths in water pollution into two career categories:

water treatment and wastewater treatment. Water treatment facilities deal with unused or "raw" water; wastewater is civic water returned to the plant for treatment after public use.

Water Treatment Jobs

Clean water doesn't flow from your faucets and shower heads by magic. Those who work with civic water supplies have a sober obligation to reliably acquire water from nearby sources, filter and treat it, and test it for toxins and impurities before pumping it through water mains to homes and businesses. The setup varies based on the water supply and the lay of the surrounding land, but many of the jobs are essentially the same.

Pump Station Operators. Treatment plants need pump station operators, whose work takes them outdoors. Water from rivers, lakes, or other sources has to be pumped to the plant and then to end users. Often millions of gallons of water are pumped daily through a series of storage tanks, conduits, and mains. The pumps are controlled by pump station operators.

All the equipment must be in good working order to allow for the proper amount of pressure, flow, and level of water for the needs of consumers. Pump station operators conduct water tests and keep records of this information. They also work with their hands and must be familiar with a variety of tools and equipment. The work can be physically demanding.

To be a pump station operator, you need a high school diploma, preferably with some experience operating and maintaining equipment. You may want to investigate two-year colleges that offer associate's degrees in environmental technology or a one-year certificate program in water quality and wastewater treatment technology. Most pollution control agencies offer continuing education courses on treatment processes, management, safety, and other subjects for workers interested in advancment.

You would probably start out as a helper or maintenance worker, during which time you would be trained. After about six months, you might advance to pump station operator and later water treatment plant operator. Most of these jobs are available at city treatment plants. The median annual salary for pump station operators in 2004 was about $34,000.

Water Treatment Plant Operators. Water treatment plant operators are similar to pump station operators, except that they maintain the purity of the water by monitoring panels to check pressure, level, and flow of the water as it moves through the pumps, adding substances to the water as needed and then testing it for purity, clarity, and odor. This operator must keep accurate records and maintain equipment.

These jobs are usually available at treatment plants in large cities and individual communities. Duties may vary according to the size of the facility, as will staff size. If you work in a very small town, your work might be only part-time. Considering all the regulations concerning water quality, however, full-time jobs will remain plentiful.

To become a water treatment plant operator, you generally need at least a high school diploma or a comparable mix of education and experience. If you've had some jobs handling machinery and mechanical equipment, so much the better. Some vocational schools offer courses in water treatment, and you can also check community colleges for environmental technology courses. The more education, training, and experience you have, the better your career opportunities will be. The median annual salary for water treatment plant operators in 2004 was about $38,000.

You might begin as an apprentice, receiving on-the-job training. Amendments to the federal Safe Drinking Water Act in the United States require certification and periodic recertification for plant operators. The exam system is tiered, so workers take more advanced tests as they progress to more responsible positions. The federal amendments lay out minimum standards; states and provinces might have stricter standards. In some cases, you may also have to update your knowledge through seminars in order to renew your license. Some states and provinces offer courses or specialized training to help you with new technology. These may include aquatic biology, new regulations, or record keeping. Check with your state or provincial licensing board for certification laws and required training. Visit the Association of Boards of Certification (www.abccert.org/links) for links to state and provincial certification pages as well as federal and association links.

Water Filter Cleaners. Another technical job in the water treatment plant is the water filter cleaner. The water filter cleaner is responsible for keeping the water clean at the bottom of the filter basin, where solids are removed from the water during the primary treatment. These basins hold layers of gravel and sand through which the water is filtered.

These filters tend to clog quickly, and the filter cleaner occasionally reverses the water flow to flush out clogs. The sand and gravel are removed with a suction pipe operated by the filter cleaner, who then hoses the sand and gravel to remove any impurities, scrapes the filter bed, and returns the clean sand and gravel to the bed. You might guess that the filter cleaner has to be physically strong—and you would be right. Filter cleaners often have to work outside the plant in sometimes less-than-comfortable surroundings.

Although this job is essential to the water purification process, it doesn't require a great deal of education, and you would receive on-the-job training. You should be reliable and industrious to tackle this kind of work. Your best employment opportunities would be with large filtration plants. This is a good entry-level job to see if you would like to become a mechanic's helper or water treatment plant operator. Water filter cleaners earned a median wage of about $14.60 per hour in 2004.

Wastewater Treatment Jobs

Many of the same processes take place for the treatment of wastewater, but in this case, sewers bring used water to the plant for cleaning and reuse. Working amidst unpleasant odors is often a daily reality. Many of these plants employ chemists, microbiologists, and a variety of other workers in addition to plant operators. Since chemists and microbiologists work mainly in laboratories, we'll concentrate on those job opportunities that are found, for the most part, outside the office or lab.

Industrial Waste Inspectors. The industrial waste inspector ensures that permits are valid and equipment up to standard and sometimes collects samples of the water for testing. He or she must go to the origin of the pollutants—the industrial or commercial site where the pollutants are treated for disposal. Any water source, such as a river, lake, or stream, has to be tested to be sure that harmful pollutants are not discharged into them from a commercial site.

Samples are also collected from sewers and drains and tested in the laboratory. Inspectors perform certain field tests on the spot, such as those for acidity and alkalinity. Most inspectors are also required to take complaints, help industry owners with compliance, and keep accurate and thorough records in order to calculate any surcharges an offending company has to pay.

As an inspector, you would be required to do quite a bit of fieldwork and would be exposed to various weather conditions. You would also do some light physical work—climbing, walking, crawling, or stretching. Because you would be looking for violations of environmental regulations, you must be able to instruct people who are responsible for following the rules while strictly enforcing those rules. You may be called on to work closely with officers of a company to educate them in federal and state regulations—which can sometimes be confusing—and help them develop solutions.

To become an industrial waste inspector, you need a good background in wastewater plant operations, an understanding of the current environmental regulations, and knowledge of equipment and machinery. Often this position is a promotion from wastewater treatment plant operator.

With further education and training, you could become a supervisor or manager. The field as a whole is stable and promising, but the best prospects will be in larger cities or industrial areas where water pollution control is most needed. The median annual salary for industrial waste inspectors in 2005 was about $44,000.

Sewer Maintenance Workers. These maintenance workers repair and maintain sewers, including manholes, storm drains, and pipes. Leaks and clogs can present real problems for civic water sanitation and wastewater return. Workers perform routine maintenance as well as replace sections that have worn out. They use a variety of power tools, high-velocity water jets, and flushers.

This job requires hard, physical labor, such as cutting trees, removing debris, and climbing into manholes. These workers have to bend, stoop, climb, kneel, and crawl in all kinds of weather in the midst of a variety of strong odors.

A high school diploma is preferred for this work, and you should count on a six-month, on-the-job training period. You could be promoted, after you have accumulated some experience, to lead worker and then to maintenance equipment operator. Earnings depend on the hours and exact nature of a city's maintenance program, but the median salary for civic sewer maintenance workers in 2005 was about $32,000.

Mechanics. Mechanics in the wastewater treatment plant are responsible for the maintenance and repair of all machines and equipment, including electric motors, turbines, pumps, and blowers. Sometimes they may operate the equipment. If you decided to become a mechanic, you'd have to be familiar with power tools, wrenches, and hoists and carry many of them with you during the workday. This requires some physical strength. The job could entail crawling, kneeling, and climbing, both inside and outside.

You would also need a high school diploma and an aptitude for mechanical work. Vocational or trade school experience is helpful, and there are apprenticeship programs available. With further education, experience, and certification, you could become the superintendent of a wastewater treatment plant. Mechanics earned a median wage of about $17 per hour in 2004.

Plant Attendants. Plant attendants adjust pipe valves, watch temperature and flow rates, turn on steam valves, and inform the superintendent of any trouble. Sometimes they are called on to collect samples and repair equipment. They may also have to perform general maintenance work, such as clearing obstructions from screens, as well as keep records. Two years of high school are sufficient for the job, with three to six months of training for an entry-level position. With further education and experience, you may qualify for certification as a wastewater treatment plant operator. The median annual salary for plant attendants in 2004 was about $30,000.

Wastewater Treatment Plant Operators. This job is similar to that of the water treatment plant operator. These workers control and operate the pumps, pipes, and valves. The flow of water and solid wastes must be monitored in order to process the proper amount of chemicals and wastewater. Pumps and generators must be stopped and started, and heat and electricity must be provided to the plant itself. In addition, all equipment must be inspected for possible repairs. This is the work of the operator.

In large plants the operators may specialize as sludge-control operators or sludge-filtration operators, for example. In other plants, operators may be called on to perform general maintenance of buildings, prepare laboratory tests, and respond to emergencies. As a plant operator, you could be working in all kinds of weather, and you might be crawling, climbing, kneeling, and crouching on the job. You would also have to know how to use common and specialized tools and be able to read blueprints.

You'd need a high school diploma, with additional consideration given for added experience in equipment maintenance. If you entered an apprenticeship program, you'd take courses in mathematics, physics, and chemistry. You might also need three years of experience in addition to this classroom training. Courses would include math, social science, computer science, communications, report writing, and wastewater treatment. In most states and provinces, you would have to pass a written test for certification. The median annual salary for plant operators in 2004 was about $36,000.

Supervisors. Supervisors are in charge of planning and coordinating all activities in the sewage system, including excavating culverts, installing sewer mains, drilling taps, and making street repairs. As a supervisor, you'd have to keep accurate records, read land plots, order materials, and maintain and repair all equipment. Much of your work would have to do with executing projects and supervising the work of others.

Most of your work would be done outdoors and demand good physical strength, eyesight, and hearing. A high school diploma is preferable, but you could rise through the ranks to become a supervisor. The median annual salary for supervisors in 2004 was about $48,000.

Technicians. Other technicians are needed in water quality control, such as the estuarine resource technician or the water pollution control technician, often called environmental engineering technicians. Estuaries, such as bays, inlets, and lagoons, need water quality monitoring because of the rich variety of wildlife they maintain. As an estuarial technician, you might have to wear diving gear to collect water samples for laboratory analysis. You would also be responsible for writing reports, working with other professionals, and operating instruments that are used in collecting samples.

A two-year associate's degree with course work in math, biology, marine instrumentation, computer science, chemistry, and English is helpful. You should also have laboratory work, ecology, and statistical analysis courses. Having a bachelor's degree would enhance your chances of being promoted.

Water pollution control technicians take samples from a variety of water sources, monitor flow and other information, operate measuring devices, and conduct on-site chemical and physical tests to help control pollutants in raw or used water. They then assemble thorough reports of this fieldwork. They often have to interpret data, prepare statistical analyses of the results, and prepare materials to be used by engineers, scientists, and environmentalists. Most of their work is done outdoors, sometimes under difficult conditions. Therefore, good physical condition is important, as is a willingness to travel a great deal.

An associate's degree in chemical technology or science is recommended. It is also important to have at least a year of experience with surveying, measuring, or testing equipment. College courses should include math, natural sciences, chemistry, biology, and engineering. You would receive training with an engineer or scientist and could advance with a bachelor's degree in engineering or science. The median annual salary for environmental engineering technicians, including estuarine resource and water pollution control technicians, was about $39,000 in 2004.

Environmental Engineering Jobs

Engineering professionals are in great demand for water quality control careers. Both government and industry are looking for environmental engineers. As an environmental engineer, you could enter the field of water pollution control, air pollution control, or solid waste management. Your job, in any case, would be to lend engineering principles and practices to environmental control systems through analysis and synthesis.

You would determine the effects of humans on natural and manmade environments—the causes and effects of all forms of pollution and the management of solid wastes. You would attempt to minimize toxic levels of waste materials through research and development of new technologies. You might work with social and applied scientists and members of the public.

You might design processes for waste treatment or figure out ways to make work environments safer. In the process, you would write reports and give presentations. You would work with a wide range of people in different areas to mutually solve problems. Therefore, your communications skills, as well as your computer and design skills, should be strong.

As an undergraduate, you might study thermodynamics, water resources, geotechnical engineering, fluid mechanics, and heat transfer. You would also probably have opportunities to solve real-life problems in laboratories to prepare you for problems you would find on the job. If you choose a career in water pollution control or solid waste management, your studies would include waste characteristics and the engineering of treatment processes and equipment. The median annual salary for environmental engineers in 2004 was about $66,500. Environmental engineers with bachelor's degrees started at an average of $47,000 in 2005.

Within the field of environmental engineering, there are a number of specialty areas for you to consider. Here are some career tracks for nature lovers who want to work in water pollution control.

Sanitary Engineers. Sanitary engineers are responsible for sewage disposal, water pollution control, or water supply problems. They also assist in watershed development and aqueduct and filtration plant construction. Sewage problems involving waste treatment plants are investigated, samples are taken, and evaluations made. These engineers may also be in charge of water supply programs for government agencies. They sometimes work at construction sites, where they advise industrial and civic leaders about wastewater treatment regulations and develop waste treatment programs.

Sanitary engineers can start by earning a bachelor's degree in civil engineering, then a master's degree in sanitary engineering. You might have chemical, structural, or public health engineering as an undergraduate major. Most states require that you be registered and licensed before you start. As a sanitary engineer, your services would be needed in private industry as a consultant to architectural firms or for major municipal wastewater treatment plants, environmental organizations, and health departments.

Hydrologic Engineers. Hydrologic engineers deal with construction of dams, aqueducts, and reservoirs for the use and control of water supplies. They study soil drainage, flooding, and conservation and analyze droughts, storms, and flood runoff records to forecast and prevent floods and plan for water storage during periods of drought. Some specialize in irrigation projects for agricultural purposes. Hydrologic engineers need a bachelor's degree in civil engineering and should have two years of experience in related work.

Oil Pollution Control Engineers. Oil pollution control engineers are responsible for prevention and control of oil spills. In worst-case scenarios, when the spill actually occurs, they plan for the cleanup and disposal of the oil. Complete prevention of oil spills may be impossible, but engineers can determine monitoring and maintenance programs for equipment and machinery and develop inspection programs for personnel to check for leaks and malfunctions. Engineers inform appropriate personnel about tides, currents, and wind patterns; they monitor those sites where oil spills might occur; and they educate gas station personnel on how to control and monitor spills in tanks, drains, and catch basins.

Plans for containment and cleanup of oil spills, once they occur, must be made individually, sometimes depending on whether they are on- or offshore, and the engineers must make decisions immediately, according to how fast the oil is dispersed and the speed of wind and current. The shape of the spill and length of time it takes to get all the contractors and helpers to the site play a role. Often training drills with a crew take place to help engineers estimate response time in case of emergency.

In the cleanup process, the engineer has many things to think about: keeping accurate records, collecting samples, working with wildlife agencies, maintaining all environmental rules and regulations, coordinating with local fire departments, and alerting local authorities to the potential threat to water sources in the affected areas. After the cleanup, the engineer arranges for disposal of the recovered oil. Some of the work would be indoors, but in emergencies, the engineers are called on to work at the site of the spill, sometimes in bad weather and unpleasant conditions.

A combination of a bachelor's degree in petroleum, chemical, or civil engineering (preferably with an emphasis on environmental engineering) and substantial experience in pollution control are necessary for a job as an oil pollution control engineer. That would qualify you to work for oil companies; contractors who specialize in cleanup; and any federal, state, or provincial agency that is responsible for the prevention, control, cleanup, and disposal of oil spills.

Civil Engineers. Civil engineers who study the physical control of water attempt to prevent floods, direct river flow, and control the water supply for irrigation purposes. If canals, locks, or hydro-electric power systems are needed, they construct them. If you choose to be a civil engineer, you would need a bachelor's degree with course work in surveying, structural engineering, hydraulics, and transportation planning in addition to basic sciences and calculus. Many programs emphasize a team approach to solving problems. The median annual salary for civil engineers in 2004 was about $64,000. Civil engineers with bachelor's degrees started at an average of $44,000 in 2005; with master's, $48,000; and with doctorates, $60,000.

More Water-Related Careers

Other careers associated with supplying water for irrigation are basin operators, ditch riders, and watershed tenders. Basin operators remove silt and sand from river water before the water enters the irrigation system. They may operate certain equipment and keep records. Ditch riders help determine how much water is needed and how long it will be needed. They often have to patrol areas to look for leaks or impediments, clear brush, or repair gauges and meters. Watershed tenders control water flow from reservoirs through the use of gauges and meters. They also keep records, maintain equipment, and solve problems.

All of these water pollution control careers—from providing quality water to controlling its flow to cleaning it up after disasters—demonstrate the importance of protecting one of our most valuable natural resources. Large numbers of professionals and technicians are needed to maintain water purity for agricultural, residential, commercial, and industrial use.

Jobs in Land Pollution Control

Land is abused in many ways on a daily basis throughout the world. One of the most pressing problems at the moment is garbage disposal. We are presently producing more solid waste than we can dispose of. The words *dumping* and *landfill* are familiar to all of us. Ordinary garbage pollutes the land and groundwater, and the contaminants are carried through the air by insects outside the dump itself. Dumps can become health hazards to humans, housing disease-carrying rodents and vermin. Even more dangerous to the land are the hazardous waste sites, which can be found throughout North America. A monumental job lies ahead for environmental professionals in disposing of such waste, containing it, or converting it to nonhazardous substances. These solid waste problems are so dangerous to the survival of our planet that it will take a concerted effort on the part of every consumer, industry, grassroots organization, environmental professional, and government agency to turn things around.

The laws on the books now are helpful, but the problem deserves the total commitment of all citizens to accomplish the kinds of results we need. In 1965, the Solid Waste Disposal Act opened the door for the development of programs that tackled the problem of disposal and provided states with financial and technical aid to carry them out. In 1980, in response to the outrage over the chemical waste disaster at Love Canal, New York, the United States Congress passed the Comprehensive Environmental Response, Compensation, and Liability Act, which established a "Superfund" for cleanup of hazardous waste sites, where the responsible parties could not be forced, or were unable, to pay. Polluting chemical industries paid into the Superfund to cover the costs of cleanup. The program worked well until Congress refused to renew the tax on polluting industries that paid for the program; funds ran out in 2003, and taxpayers have since assumed responsibility for funding cleanups, leading to slashed budgets and delays. Time will tell whether changing political fortunes will lead to the "polluter pays" funding being reinstated.

Canada has the Canadian Environmental Protection Act, passed in 1988 and revised in 1999, which identifies and regulates disposal of toxic substances that could threaten the public health and that of the environment. Another act, the Transportation of Dangerous Goods Act, passed in 1980, restricts the transport of hazardous waste both within Canada and across international borders. At the time of its passage, industries in developed countries were causing problems by unloading their hazardous waste in poorer countries that were unable to handle it properly.

As expanding populations have moved closer to the potential sites for landfills and waste disposal sites, citizens have become more aware of the problems associated with trash and toxic waste. In the United States the rush to migrate west has made sites such as Yucca Mountain, the proposed site for permanent storage of the country's nuclear waste, much less remote. People are demanding solutions based on individual and corporate accountability, not a handoff to a third party or government agency. Many communities now offer single-stream recycling that allows its residents to return a large portion of their household waste, such as cardboard and coated paper, for processing and reuse. Sanitary landfills have become the norm, so that solid waste is disposed of within layers and then covered over to reduce pollutants. Consumers are demanding of manufacturers that they reduce their packaging, and scientists, leading thinkers, and celebrities are spurring a green revolution.

Waste Management Engineers

Careers with solid waste management and hazardous waste cleanup are numerous, and the field is growing, just as the waste problem is. At the forefront are waste management engineers, who study specifications and plans, inspect disposal facilities, recommend ways to process and dispose of garbage, and develop resource-recovery programs. They write reports and advise the appropriate people in government or industry on rules and regulations regarding waste disposal.

A combination of a bachelor's degree in engineering and work experience in waste management or a master's degree in waste management engineering will qualify you for a position in this field. The median annual salary for waste management engineers was about $48,000 in 2006.

Waste Management Specialists

Alongside the engineers are the waste management specialists. Although they don't design programs, they inspect landfills, confer with appropriate health officials, advise those who operate sanitary landfills about improved methods of disposal, take complaints, and prepare reports. You could qualify for this position with a bachelor's degree in environmental science or civil, sanitary, or chemical engineering. Some experience in solid waste management is preferred. The median annual salary for waste management specialists was about $42,000 in 2006.

Jobs in Air Pollution Control

Air pollution is a hot topic in many environmental circles. Overall air quality has been improving for years—witness notoriously smoggy California's leadership in restricting automobile emissions and investing in wind and solar technology—but much remains to be done. Scientists have learned how damaging fine-particulate matter can be to people's lungs, particularly in children and the elderly, and air pollution easily crosses international borders and can bring acid rain, plant devastation, and lots of controversy with it. As scientists better understand what damage air pollution causes and technology allows us to curb it, the field will need more researchers and regulators to manage the problem.

Air Quality Engineers

If you are feeling committed enough to explore the career possibilities in air quality and pollution control, know that the need for environmental professionals is great and will be in the future. For example, air quality engineers are needed in governmental agencies, private industry, oil refineries, electric power plants, and consulting firms. Their responsibilities include visiting industrial sites, investigating trouble areas, making recommendations for improvements, and setting deadlines for compliance. They also plan new construction, with pollution reduction a primary objective. These plans may be for commercial plants, power plants, or highways. They consider traffic patterns, climate, housing density, and even wind direction when making recommendations for new construction.

Some air quality engineers design testing devices, devise new pollution-reducing processes, or explore ways to remove pollutants from certain substances. They work indoors and outdoors, are on call in emergencies, and have the ability to solve problems and do research. Many travel to specific sites on a regular basis and often have to climb, lift, and otherwise perform physical tasks in various climate conditions.

To qualify as an air quality engineer, you need a bachelor's degree in engineering and certification as a professional engineer. If you want to work for the government, you must pass the civil service exam. The median annual salary for air quality engineers was about $57,000 in 2006.

Chemical Engineers

Chemical engineers, like environmental and civil engineers, are in demand in both government and industry, helping to solve air pollution control problems. They work in the manufacturing, pharmaceutical, biotechnology, and environmental safety industries. Among government agencies that hire chemical engineers are the Environmental Protection Agency and the departments of the Interior, Commerce, and Agriculture; the U.S. Army; and the Nuclear Regulatory Commission. Chemical engineers need a college or university degree, with grounding in the sciences, math, and computers. The median annual salary for chemical engineers was about $77,000 in 2004. Chemical engineers started at an average of $54,000 with a bachelor's degree in 2005, $57,000 with a master's, and $80,000 with a doctorate.

Air Quality Specialists

Air quality specialists go into the field to inspect, test, and analyze pollution sources, take samples of soil and other materials affected by air pollution, and write reports and recommendations. They prepare environmental impact statements, take complaints on hazards caused by toxic waste, and assist in enforcing environmental protection regulations.

A bachelor's degree in science, engineering, environmental health, or statistics is necessary to qualify you for work as an air quality specialist. You should study chemistry, physics, and biology as an undergraduate.

Knowledge of computers, public administration, and environmental studies is also beneficial. You would probably also receive on-the-job training, whether you worked for the government, industry, or consulting firms. The median annual salary for air quality specialists was about $51,000 in 2006.

Air Quality Technicians

Air quality technicians assist engineers and scientists by collecting air samples, testing them for pollutants, and recording the information. They inspect pollution sources and operate electronic equipment. Much of this work is done on site and often involves repairing equipment, drawing graphs, and solving equations.

You may prefer to specialize in meteorological work as an air quality technician. In that case, you would work with meteorologists in forecasting levels of air pollution. You would work at test sites to check equipment and record temperatures, wind velocity and direction, and air pressure. You would assist the meteorologist in setting up weather instruments, performing mathematical calculations, and working with maps and graphs. This would require two years of college or technical training, including laboratory, mechanical, and electrical experience. You would also have to be well versed in air quality regulations. The median annual salary for environmental engineering technicians was about $39,000 in 2004.

....

Scholarships, Fellowships, and Student Training

In the United States, the Environmental Protection Agency and various nonprofit organizations provide a range of opportunities and resources that are available to undergraduate college students, graduate students, and others seeking experience to break into the environmental field through its Office of Environmental Education (www.epa.gov/enviroed).

The National Network for Environmental Management Studies (NNEMS), one EPA program, offers students fellowships for practical research experiences that allow them to work during the summer or during the school year. Fellowships are in environmental policy, regulation, and law; environmental management and administration; environmental science; public relations and communications; and computer programming and development. Fellowships are awarded to eligible undergraduate and graduate students. Visit the website at www.epa.gov/enviroed/NNEMS for more information.

Another EPA program targeting talented young people is its National Center for Environmental Research (NCER; http://es .epa.gov/ncer), which seeks to motivate students for careers in the environment and to enhance the work of practicing environmentalists with visiting scientist programs. The NCER provides research grants and fellowships.

The EPA also sponsors the Environmental Careers Organization's (ECO) Diversity Initiative, a program to introduce underrepresented groups to environmental careers while increasing opportunities for them. ECO's programs, open to students of all races and ethnic backgrounds, include the Conservation Careers Diversity Program for internships with the U.S. Fish and Wildlife Service and U.S. Forest Service, the EPA Community Intern Program, and the EPA Greater Research Opportunities (GRO) Fellowship, which comes with a two-year scholarship and a summer internship with the EPA. Visit www.eco.org for more information. Canada has a similar organization, known as ECO Canada (www.eco.ca), which brings together qualified students with interested employers through internships, career resources, and certification.

The American Indian Science and Engineering Society (www.aises.org) offers scholarships for students in engineering and the hard sciences and internships with the federal government, including the National Science Foundation, the Centers for Disease Control and Prevention, and the Bonneville Power Administration in Portland, Oregon. The students are judged on such criteria as grade point average, knowledge of their culture, intent to work for the environment, and leadership.

The Canadian government runs the Science Horizons Youth Internship Program (www.ec.gc.ca/sci_hor), an initiative undertaken with help from Canadian universities and nonprofits to connect undergraduate and graduate students with workplace experience in areas such as ecosystem research and wildlife research and management while in school. Internships last from six months to one year, with the program cycle beginning in April and ending in March.

As you can see from these types of structured educational opportunities, and from the programs outlined in previous chapters, there are plenty of people already active in outdoor careers who want to see you succeed, too. Hiring managers everywhere are contemplating who will appear to carry the torch of environmental leadership for the next generation. Now is the time for you to decide what contribution you could make and where you will best fit. Once you do, there is an army of professionals and other resources that can help you decide on next steps. (Also see the Appendix on the following pages for further information.) The better educated and informed you are, the better your chance of finding a good and lasting career in the outdoor field of your choice. Congratulations on taking the first step!

Career Resources

Job Sites

Many professional associations and nonprofits have public or members-only job boards. Be sure to check out the sites listed in those sections as well for additional leads and information.

BiologyJobs.Com
www.biologyjobs.com

CareerBuilder.com
www.careerbuilder.com

EcoEmploy.com
www.ecoemploy.com

Federal Jobs Digest
www.jobsfed.com

Federal Research Service
www.fedjobs.com

JobBank
www.jobbank.gc.ca

Monster.com
www.monster.com

Naturejobs.com
www.naturejobs.nature.com

Public Service Commission of Canada
www.jobs-emplois.gc.ca

ScienceCareers.org (*Science* magazine and American
  Association for the Advancement of Science)
http://sciencecareers.sciencemag.org

ScienceJobs.com (*New Scientist Magazine*)
www.sciencejobs.com

U.S. Office of Personnel Management
www.usajobs.gov

Vault
www.vault.com

Yahoo! HotJobs
www.hotjobs.yahoo.com

Professional Associations

American Association for the Advancement of Science
1200 New York Avenue NW
Washington, DC 20005
www.aaas.org

American Association of Petroleum Geologists
PO Box 979
Tulsa, OK 74101
www.aapg.org

American Association of Zoo Keepers, Inc.
3601 Southwest Twenty-Ninth Street, Suite 133
Topeka, KS 66614
www.aazk.org

American Association of Zoo Veterinarians
581705 White Oak Road
Yulee, FL 32097
www.aazv.org

American Fisheries Society
5410 Grosvenor Lane
Bethesda, MD 20814
www.fisheries.org

American Geological Institute
4220 King Street
Alexandria, VA 22302
www.agiweb.org

American Geophysical Union
2000 Florida Avenue NW
Washington, DC 20009
www.agu.org

American Institute of Biological Sciences
1444 I Street NW, Suite 200
Washington, DC 20005
www.aibs.org

American Institute of Chemical Engineers
3 Park Avenue
New York, NY 10016
www.aiche.org

American Ornithologists' Union
1313 Dolley Madison Boulevard, Suite 402
McLean, VA 22101
www.aou.org

American Planning Association
122 South Michigan Avenue, Suite 1600
Chicago, IL 60603
www.planning.org

American Society of Agronomy
677 South Segoe Road
Madison, WI 53711
www.agronomy.org

American Society of Landscape Architects
636 Eye Street NW
Washington, DC 20001
www.asla.org

American Society for Microbiology
1752 N Street NW
Washington, DC 20036
www.asm.org

American Veterinary Medical Association
1931 North Meacham Road, Suite 100
Schaumburg, IL 60173
www.avma.org

Association of American Geographers
1710 Sixteenth Street NW
Washington, DC 20009
www.aag.org

Association of American Veterinary Medical Colleges
1101 Vermont Avenue NW, Suite 301
Washington, DC 20005
www.aavmc.org

Association for Experiential Education
3775 Iris Avenue, Suite 4
Boulder, CO 80301
www.aee.org

Association of Zoos & Aquariums
8403 Colesville Road, Suite 710
Silver Spring, MD 20910
www.aza.org

Biotechnology Industry Organization (BIO)
1201 Maryland Avenue SW, Suite 900
Washington, DC 20024
www.bio.org

Botanical Society of America
PO Box 299
St. Louis, MO 63166
www.botany.org

Canadian Institute of Forestry
504-151 Slater Street
Ottawa, ON K1P 5H3
Canada
www.cif-ifc.org

Canadian Society of Landscape Architects
PO Box 13594
Ottawa, ON K2K 1X6
Canada
www.csla.ca

Canadian Society of Zoologists
www.csz-scz.ca

Canadian Veterinarian Medical Association
339 Booth Street
Ottawa, ON K1R 7K1
Canada
www.canadianveterinarians.net

Crop Science Society of America
677 South Segoe Road
Madison, WI 53711
www.crops.org

ECO Canada
308 Eleventh Avenue SE, Suite 200
Calgary, AL T2G 0Y2
Canada
www.eco.ca

Ecological Society of America
1707 H Street NW, Suite 400
Washington, DC 20006
www.esa.org

Entomological Society of America
10001 Derekwood Lane, Suite 100
Lanham, MD 20706
www.entsoc.org

Environmental Careers Organization
30 Winter Street, Sixth Floor
Boston, MA 02108
www.eco.org

Geological Association of Canada
Department of Earth Sciences
Alexander Murray Building, Room ER4063
Memorial University of Newfoundland
St. John's, NL A1B 3X5
Canada
www.gac.ca

Geological Society of America
PO Box 9140
Boulder, CO 80301
www.geosociety.org

Institute of Food Technologists
525 West Van Buren, Suite 1000
Chicago, IL 60607
www.ift.org

Marine Technology Society
5565 Sterrett Place, Suite 108
Columbia, MD 21044
www.mtsociety.org

National Association of Biology Teachers
12030 Sunrise Valley Drive, Suite 110
Reston, VA 20191
www.nabt.org

National Association of Federal Veterinarians
1910 Sunderland Place NW
Washington, DC 20036
www.nafv.org

National Association of State Foresters
Hall of the States
444 North Capitol Street NW, Suite 540
Washington, DC 20001
www.stateforesters.org

The Oceanography Society
PO Box 1931
Rockville, MD 20849
www.tos.org

Society of American Foresters
5400 Grosvenor Lane
Bethesda, MD 20814
www.safnet.org

Society of Exploration Geophysicists
PO Box 702740
Tulsa, OK 74170
www.seg.org

Society for Range Management
10030 West Twenty-Seventh Avenue
Wheat Ridge, CO 80215
www.rangelands.org

Soil Science Society of America
677 South Segoe Road
Madison, WI 53711
www.soils.org

University-National Oceanographic Laboratory System
Moss Landing Marine Laboratories
8272 Moss Landing Road
Moss Landing, CA 95039
www.unols.org

Wilson Ornithological Society
Museum of Zoology
University of Michigan
Ann Arbor, MI 48109
www.ummz.umich.edu/birds/wos/index.html

Conservation Associations

American Bird Conservancy
PO Box 249
The Plains, VA 20198
www.abcbirds.org

Bird Studies Canada
PO Box 160
Port Rowan, ON N0E 1M0
Canada
www.bsc-eoc.org

Farm Animal Reform Movement (FARM)
10101 Ashburton Lane
Bethesda, MD 20817
www.farmusa.org

Fellow Mortals
W4632 Palmer Road
Lake Geneva, WI 53147
www.fellowmortals.org

Greenpeace
702 H Street NW
Washington, DC 20001
www.greenpeace.org

Humane Farming Association
PO Box 3577
San Rafael, CA 94912
www.hfa.org

National Audubon Society
700 Broadway
New York, NY 10003
www.audubon.org

National Fish and Wildlife Foundation
1120 Connecticut Avenue NW, Suite 900
Washington, DC 20036
www.nfwf.org

National Wildlife Federation
11100 Wildlife Center Drive
Reston, VA 20190
www.nwf.org

Nature Conservancy
4245 North Fairfax Drive, Suite 100
Arlington, VA 22203
www.nature.org

Sierra Club
85 Second Street, Second Floor
San Francisco, CA 94105
www.sierraclub.org

Soil and Water Conservation Society
945 Southwest Ankeny Road
Ankeny, IA 50023
www.swcs.org

Student Conservation Association
PO Box 550
Charlestown, NH 03603
www.thesca.org

Wilderness Society
1615 M Street NW
Washington, DC 20036
www.wilderness.org

Wildlife Management Institute
1146 Nineteenth Street NW, Suite 700
Washington, DC 20036
www.wildlifemanagementinstitute.org

Government-Related Resources

Agriculture and Agri-Food Canada
Sir John Carling Building
930 Carling Avenue
Ottawa, ON K1A 0C7
Canada
www.agr.gc.ca

Bureau of Indian Affairs
1849 C Street NW
Washington, DC 20240
www.doi.gov/bureau-indian-affairs.html

Canada Centre for Remote Sensing
588 Booth Street
Ottawa, ON K1A 0Y7
Canada
www.ccrs.nrcan.gc.ca

Canadian Environmental Assessment Agency
Twenty-Second Floor, Place Bell
160 Elgin Street
Ottawa, ON K1A 0H3
Canada
www.ceaa-acee.gc.ca

Canadian Forest Service
Natural Resources Canada
580 Booth Street, Eighth Floor
Ottawa, ON K1A 0E4
Canada
www.cfs.nrcan.gc.ca

Canadian Waters
Fisheries and Oceans Canada
Communications Branch
200 Kent Street
Thirteenth Floor, Station 13228
Ottawa, ON K1A 0E6
Canada
www.dfo-mpo.gc.ca

Canadian Wildlife Service
Environment Canada
Ottawa, ON K1A 0H3
Canada
www.cws-scf.ec.gc.ca

Centers for Disease Control and Prevention
1600 Clifton Road
Atlanta, GA 30333
www.cdc.gov

Consumer Product Safety Commission
4330 East West Highway
Bethesda, MD 20814
www.cpsc.gov

Convention on Biological Diversity
Secretariat
413 Saint Jacques Street, Suite 800
Montreal, QC H2Y 1N9
Canada
www.biodiv.org

Council on Environmental Quality
722 Jackson Place NW
Washington, DC 20503
www.whitehouse.gov/ceq

Environment Canada
Inquiry Centre
70 Crémazie Street
Gatineau, QC K1A 0H3
Canada
www.ec.gc.ca

Federal Aviation Administration
800 Independence Avenue SW
Washington, DC 20591
www.faa.gov

Federal Highway Administration
400 Seventh Street SW
Washington, DC 20590
www.fhwa.gov

Geological Survey of Canada
Natural Resources Canada
360-601 Booth Street
Ottawa, ON K1A 0E8
Canada
www.gsc.nrcan.gc.ca

Health Canada
775 Brookfield Road
AL 6302C
Ottawa, ON K1A 1C1
Canada
www.hc-sc.gc.ca

National Geospatial-Intelligence Agency
Public Affairs Division, MS D-54
4600 Sangamore Road
Bethesda, MD 20816
www.nga.mil

National Marine Fisheries Service
1315 East West Highway, Ninth Floor
Silver Spring, MD 20910
www.nmfs.noaa.gov

National Park Service
1849 C Street NW
Washington, DC 20240
www.nps.gov

Natural Resources Conservation Service
1400 Independence Avenue SW
Washington, DC 20250
www.nrcs.usda.gov

Occupational Safety & Health Administration
200 Constitution Avenue NW
Washington, DC 20210
www.osha.gov

Parks Canada
25 Eddy Street
Gatineau, QC K1A 0M5
Canada
www.pc.gc.ca

Pest Management Regulatory Agency
2720 Riverside Drive
AL 6606D2
Ottawa, ON K1A 0K9
Canada
www.pmra-aria.gc.ca

Public Service Commission of Canada
Staffing and Assessment Services Branch
66 Slater Street, Fourth Floor
Ottawa, ON K1A 0M7
Canada
www.jobs-emplois.gc.ca

Tennessee Valley Authority
400 West Summit Hill Drive
Knoxville, TN 37902
www.tva.com

U.S. Bureau of Land Management
Office of Public Affairs
1849 C Street, Room 406-LS
Washington, DC 20240
www.blm.gov

U.S. Bureau of Reclamation
1849 C Street NW
Washington, DC 20240
www.usbr.gov

U.S. Census Bureau
4600 Silver Hill Road
Washington, DC 20233
www.census.gov

U.S. Department of Agriculture
1400 Independence Avenue SW
Washington, DC 20250
www.usda.gov

U.S. Department of Commerce
1401 Constitution Avenue NW
Washington, DC 20230
www.commerce.gov

U.S. Department of Energy
1000 Independence Avenue SW
Washington, DC 20585
www.doe.gov

U.S. Department of the Interior
1849 C Street NW
Washington, DC 20240
www.doi.gov

U.S. Department of Transportation
400 Seventh Street SW
Washington, DC 20590
www.dot.gov

U.S. Fish and Wildlife Service
1849 C Street NW
Washington, DC 20240
www.fws.gov

U.S. Food and Drug Administration
5600 Fishers Lane
Rockville, MD 20857
www.fda.gov

U.S. Forest Service
1400 Independence Avenue SW
Washington, DC 20250
www.fs.fed.us

U.S. Geological Survey
USGS National Center
12201 Sunrise Valley Drive
Reston, VA 20192
www.usgs.gov

U.S. Office of Personnel Management
1900 E Street NW
Washington, DC 20415
www.usajobs.gov

Corporate Resources

Amgen
One Amgen Center Drive
Thousand Oaks, CA 91320
www.amgen.com

Dow Chemical Company
2030 Dow Center
Midland, MI 48674
www.dow.com

About the Author

In addition to her love of nature, Louise Miller loves languages, especially English and German. She started out as a German teacher in various colleges and universities, and she continues to tutor today. She has studied in Vienna, Austria, and Bonn, Germany.

Her love of English led her to teaching, writing, editing, and proofreading. She has taught English at community and business colleges, has conducted writing workshops, and has worked both full-time and freelance for a variety of publishing houses. These include Compton's Encyclopedia, Rand McNally & Company, World Book, and School Zone.

Other books Miller has written in this series are *Careers for Animal Lovers & Other Zoological Types* and *Careers for Night Owls & Other Insomniacs*. Children's books include *Career Portraits: Animals* and *Turkey: Between East and West*. Miller is a contributing writer for Rand McNally's book, *America*. She is currently working as the marketing and communications manager for a nonprofit organization.